Time For
Wonderlust™

Time For Wonderlust™

PLANNING YOUR RETIREMENT RENAISSANCE

FORREST J. WRIGHT

Time for Wonderlust: Planning Your Retirement Renaissance
©2018 Forrest J. Wright

Publisher's Cataloging-In-Publication Data
(Prepared by The Donohue Group, Inc.)

Names: Wright, Forrest J.
Title: Time for wonderlust : planning your retirement renaissance / Forrest J. Wright.
Description: [Farmington, Connecticut] : Real Leisure Press, [2017] | Includes bibliographical references and index.
Identifiers: ISBN 978-0-9969451-2-7 (print) | ISBN 978-0-9969451-3-4 (ebook)
Subjects: LCSH: Retirement--Planning. | Retirees--Conduct of life. | Aging--Philosophy.
Classification: LCC HQ1062 .W75 2017 (print) | LCC HQ1062 (ebook) | DDC 646.79--dc23

Cover Design: 1106 Design

Book Shepherd: Shel Horowitz

ISBNs:
Print: 978-0-9969451-0-3
eBook: 978-0-9969451-3-4

Printed in the United States of America

10 9 8 7 6 5 4 3 2 1

Library of Congress Control Number: 2016940954

Published by Real Leisure Press

This book is dedicated to my late father, whose name my son and I bear. The only physical item in his will left specifically to me was a small stuffed bear from Tibet that he believed was once a Yeti. That bear travelled with me through four moves, usually ending up in the basement. It took me many years to realize what he left me was not a stuffed animal but his wonderlust.

CONTENTS

INTRODUCTION

During my working years, I dreamed of saving so much money that I could retire early and pursue a better life—a life of culture and meaningful leisure. They say money can't buy happiness, but I believe if you save enough, you can buy the leisure time to find it.

Philosopher John Stuart Mill defined happiness simply as a condition of "intended pleasure and the absence of pain" (*Utilitarianism*, 1871). He added that intelligent men who had experienced both the pleasures of the mind and pleasures of the senses have reported enjoying the former more. "Better to be a Socrates dissatisfied than a fool satisfied." Often, though, the circumstances of life have left us with only the pleasures of the fool. As Mill tells us in *Utilitarianism*:

> Capacity for nobler feelings is in most natures a very tender plant . . . and in a majority of young persons it speedily dies away if the occupations to which their positions in life have devoted them . . .are not favorable to keeping that higher capacity in exercise. Men lose their higher aspirations as they lose their intellectual tastes, because they have not the time or opportunity to indulge them.

When we're young, we work because we must, but in return we expect free time to pursue our deeper interests. "We work in order to be at leisure." (Aristotle, *Nicomachean Ethics*). But, steadily, the demands of work, the cost of status, and our responsibilities all creep up on us. And we have less energy for activities outside of work and family. Free time, too, becomes a servant to work: We need time to recuperate from today's work and to steel ourselves for tomorrow's grind. We tune out for a couple of hours with low-commitment entertainments like television, the Internet, and other digital avenues. After a while, we no longer remember what those deeper interests were.

> [The] get-rich-quick disease of my youth spread like wildfire. It produced a civilization which has destroyed simplicity and repose of life, its poetry, its soft romantic dreams and visions, and replaced them with a money fever, sordid ideals, vulgar ambitions, and the sleep which does not refresh. It created a thousand useless luxuries and turned them into necessities, and satisfied nothing. It has dethroned God and set up a shekel in his place. Oh, the dreams of our youth—how beautiful they are, and how perishable!
>
> —Mark Twain, portrayed by Hal Holbrook
> Mark Twain Tonight (CBS–1967)

Others around me didn't share my dream of cultural leisure. After trying to research the subject, I began to see two main reasons why Americans preferred more time at work to more time in leisure. First, our need for the social status of conspicuous consumption drives us to work and spend as much money as we possibly can. With little incentive to build larger savings from a low-cost lifestyle, early retirement is impossible. Second, we generally don't see a future of intellectual leisure as an attractive alternative to the obvious joys of shopping and spending in the present. Pleasures of the mind have lost out to pleasures of the senses.

I didn't achieve early retirement but saved enough for a consolation prize of being my own boss for the last sixteen years of my career. Finally, in retirement I began to write about the obstacles to early retirement and a life of leisure. Part way into this project, it struck me that I was not addressing an obvious question: What exactly was my hoped-for payoff from a life of leisure? This was something I had not yet articulated. Pertaining to that payoff, though, I did have two clues. First, I was convinced, because of certain wonderful, but brief, episodes in my life, that there was something better out there for me, just out of sight, that I was meant to find. Second, the discipline that claimed to operate at the outer borders of knowledge, and might help me find this something, was philosophy. This book is my journey following these clues and learning about the pleasures of the mind.

> If you take out of life the few moments of religion, art, and pure love, what is left but a series of trivial thoughts?
>
> —Arthur Schopenhauer (age 20)

Have you ever experienced a surprisingly sublime moment, clearly disconnected from everyday life, when you felt awe and wonder and at peace with the world? Researchers have studied these experiences and have concluded most of us have had at least one of these episodes in our lives. The vast majority of people will write them off as just "having a good day" and give it little thought.[1] But, what if there were more to it? Many people have said their experiences conveyed to them a strong sense of authenticity; they were *more real than their normal life*. My belief is that these episodes provide a free glimpse into a better reality, which I refer to as transcendence. Imagine yourself working your way through a drab career maze in rat-race fashion when you happen to pass a

---

1 "Men occasionally stumble over the truth, but most of them pick themselves up and hurry off as if nothing had happened." Winston Churchill. *Reader's Digest* (1942).

window with a view of a beautiful landscape. You have to keep moving, but you don't forget the view. Can you ever find your way back to that landscape?

In finding our way back to youthful idealism, we need first to understand what led us astray and left us unable financially to afford a real retirement. This I put at the feet of status seeking and the resulting need for maximum work (Chapters 1 and 2). But, few in our society speak any more about alternatives to work, so the historical concept of leisure needs to be re-introduced (Chapter 3).

STATUS & LEISURE

CHAPTER ONE

WORK, STATUS AND TIME

Sometimes, as I drift idly on Walden Pond,
I cease to live and begin to be.

—Henry David Thoreau

F or most Americans, classical philosophical leisure simply cannot compete in the market for time with the bounties of work. If people worked only long enough to provide for their basic needs, then there could be time for both. But they work well beyond that. Virtually every time in the last century Americans, as a nation or as individual groups, have had a choice between shorter working hours or making more money, they've chosen the latter.

It's not greed that propels their preference for work and consumption, but rather, status seeking. Status is an enormously powerful motivator against which the charms of classical leisure can't compete. In our celebrity-mad world, it's like comparing the relative attractiveness of a superstar, say Angelina Jolie, against the local bag lady.

This chapter tries to level the playing field by showing how leisure is misunderstood and by exposing some of the wastefulness of an unbridled pursuit of status. I'm trying to give the bag lady a makeover and reveal some of the warts and cosmetic tricks of the superstar.

Aren't all Americans seeking success? We all have certain advantages and disadvantages bestowed by our national and ethnic origins, our parents' genes and upbringing, and by input from others in the community. This is the hand we were dealt.

Americans seek to trump that hand by rising further in their education and careers or by accumulating more wealth and fame than expected. It matters little if we are a hundred times wealthier than our counterparts in Uganda. What does matter is how wealthy we are compared to others in our community. Yet most will probably not significantly surpass their heritage, especially those born to upper middle-class families. But we feel compelled to ensure that we at least hold on to our relative position on the community's totem pole. Status is our relative placement in prestige and wealth in our community.

In a status-seeking world, leisure or free-time activities are usually evaluated in terms of their contribution to status. If you develop expertise in a hobby, you may become well-known among certain groups and thereby add to your general status. Or, you might take exotic vacations, buy a vacation home, or entertain lavishly. These free-time activities could add to a reputation of wealth. Even watching sports on television can be seen to help status indirectly by rejuvenating the worker for a successful return to the competitive world of work and to hold one's own in social conversations about sports around the water cooler.

But what about a leisure which has nothing to do with status but everything to do with transcendence? Perhaps leisure could mean studying philosophy, religion, and other humanities. Immediately, though, the age-old question arises: What is the value? For example, what if you learned French, using Rosetta Stone software, and told no one? You weren't planning to go to France soon or need French for work. What's the value in that? Obviously, there's no status value. It would have to have its own intrinsic value. For philosophy and religion, that value might be to have a sense of place and meaning in the universe and an inkling of a reality beyond the well-trodden and well-lit pathways of our everyday life.

STANLEY WAS DEEPLY DISAPPOINTED WHEN, HIGH IN THE TIBETAN MOUNTAINS, HE FINALLY FOUND HIS TRUE SELF.

Reprinted with permission of Chris Madden at chris@chrismadden.co.uk

WHAT'S YOUR STATUS?

> [The needs of human beings] . . . fall into two classes—those
> needs which are absolute in the sense that we feel them whatever the
> situation of our fellow beings may be, and those which are relative
> only in that their satisfaction lifts us above, makes us superior to, our
> fellows. . . . [Those] second class needs may indeed be insatiable; for
> the higher the general level, the higher still are they.
>
> —John Maynard Keynes
> *Essays in Persuasion*, (1931, p. 365)

The terms "conspicuous consumption," "status seekers," and "keeping up
with the Joneses" are such accepted parts of the American lexicon that their
mention barely raises an eyebrow. We all recognize the illogic or the inefficiency
of chasing status. After all, Thorstein Veblen, who coined the term "conspicuous consumption," pointed this out more than 100 years ago. But nothing in
those 100-plus years has slowed our innate drive for status.

So why bother re-examining the issue? Because the side effects have reached
alarmingly high levels. One side effect is the cost in time of status seeking,
which has driven other uses of time off the marketplace. Another side effect
is the large increase in the use of sweatshops in underdeveloped countries and
factory farms required to support our conspicuous consumption. The planet is
now threatened with global warming and the depletion of natural resources.
Finally, there is the recent realization that just maintaining a middle-class
lifestyle status, including a home and college education for the children, has
forced many citizens to take on uncomfortable levels of debt, thereby desta-
bilizing the economy. These latter two side effects will *not* be addressed here
but are the subject of extensive treatment elsewhere. Time loss, however, is
not much discussed anywhere and *is* addressed in this chapter.

Those Joneses we compete with for status, unfortunately, keep getting richer. That means the cost of relative status has risen, too. Americans have to work longer hours and spend more time attending to their conspicuous consumption. This is the time spent shopping, using the acquisitions, and maintaining them. The classic example of increased consumption of time is the day you buy a home in the suburbs. From that day forward, you'll need to spend several extra hours a week on longer commutes to and from work and on tasks such as mowing the lawn and shoveling the driveway.

Not only does consumption time increase with a new home, but home-owners must also work longer hours to continue to afford it. Juliet Schor has documented that the average workweek increased four hours per worker from 1973 to 2000. The effect on couples, whose workweek has increased a combined eight hours, has been more dramatic. As relative status needs have grown, nonworking wives have had to enter the workforce. Additionally, child and home care chores, formerly done by the stay-at-home wife, are now shared, cutting into the husband's free time. Ms. Schor's survey respondents complain that they are left with only sixteen and a half hours of free time per week.[2]

They have themselves to blame. If, instead of trading their gains in work productivity since 1970 for more income and consumption, they had opted for cuts in working hours, they could now be enjoying a much more leisurely lifestyle. Perhaps, there could even have been enough free time for cultural leisure. Ms. Schor has estimated hypothetically how far the cuts could have gone: "The normal workweek could go as low as 20 hours, plus seven weeks of vacation." (p. 11) But, that would have meant no extra consumption. For example, it might have meant continuing to live in a 1970-style home of 1400 square feet, compared to today's average of 2400 square feet (based on the Census Bureau's estimates for new single-family homes). By the way, the greater space has largely been driven by the need for more storage.

---

2 *Take Back Your Time*, John de Graaf, Editor, 2003.

Schor, John de Graaf, and others point out how overworked Americans are, leading to high stress and hectic lifestyles with little time for recreation. Their books can be fascinating reading, but one is left wondering why, despite their convincing analysis, nothing changes.

I believe there are two reasons. First, no one has defined a meaningful alternative to work that matches the significant benefits of work. Conceptually, the week is still divided into work and "not-work." And "not-work" is not all that attractive. As one of Studs Terkel's co-workers complains: Time off with the wife was "honey dew" time: "Honey, do this" and "Honey, do that." Some writers who decry the obsession with work suggest more time off could be better used with family activities or doing volunteer work. Others suggest status-related recreation like home improvement or golf. They are all worthy activities, but they are also responsibility or status-driven.[3] In fact, too much free time is quite frightening to some. "One must work . . . since . . . to work is less wearisome than to amuse oneself."[4]

The second reason for lack of change in America's overworked condition is that those writing about it haven't explained this obsession with work and consumption. Of course, they recognize that Americans work hard to maintain

---

3　When analyzed from the viewpoint of status, free-time activities can be put in different categories, ranging from useless to almost exemplary. Contemplative leisure falls in the useless category, along with lollygagging and killing time. It does nothing to enhance one's status, unless by a miracle you become a published poet. At best, it doesn't carry negative status, like becoming a drug addict. Not-quite-so-useless free-time activities are ones that, while not social or competitive, may renew you for work like watching soap operas, reading romance novels, pursuing nonproductive hobbies, and engaging in solitary exercise. Similar activities, but with more challenge and done with social goals in mind, are seen as more positive status aids. Examples are watching sports to share with office workers, reading best-sellers for discussion at a book club, and joining an exercise class. Finally, there are some exemplary free-time pursuits that absolutely boost status. Golf is at the top of the list. It can build useful business contacts with heavy hitters, open access to exclusive clubs, and build one's athletic reputation—universally recognized through the handicap convention. Tennis is a poor cousin to golf but almost as good. Then there's sailing, skiing, exotic vacations, and vacation homes. They provide useful avenues for exclusivity and conspicuous consumption. As income increases and free time becomes scarce, the less status-related activities, like contemplation, are jettisoned first.

4　Charles Baudelaire, *Intimate Journals*, 1930

or advance their lifestyle. But why is that lifestyle so critically important? Couldn't Americans reduce their consumption-craving a little to gain a couple of hours of stress-free time? Instead, Americans march onward, working an average of nine more hours a year, year after year, while dreaming of the day they will retire and lie on a sunny beach.[5]

My belief is that the true cause for overwork is the need for status, not a desire for more consumption, per se. And, this need for status is more basic and more ingrained than is generally recognized.

The only writer I'm aware of who truly explained the desire for over-consumption is Thorstein Veblen.[6] He traces the causes back to the dawn of civilized man, suggesting that conspicuous consumption is a survival trait deep in our unconscious, part of our pre-history psyche.

As our ancestors settled down from a migratory life into tribes of hunter-gatherers, they changed from a relatively classless society to a more vertically structured one. There was division of labor between those who grew, gathered, and prepared food, and those who hunted game and acted as warriors and defenders of the tribe from invaders. The gatherer class was usually females

---

5 *How to Love Your Retirement*, by Barbara Waxman and Robert A. Mendelson, 2006, includes a small survey on which activity seniors mention first when asked about what they do or plan to do in retirement. Many responders seem motivated by a need to justify the use of their free time, prefacing their answers with the statement that they "have never been busier." By far, the largest category of primary activities is related to work. Volunteer work 15, part-time work 14, self-employment 10, new career 4, and work till I drop 3. Also listed was work around the home: gardening, home repair, and yard work. I assume these work activities were motivated by either financial need or the desire to engage in useful activities. The second most mentioned activities (perhaps 15 total) were related to sports like golf, tennis, swimming, skiing, walking, and dancing. A couple mentioned intellectual pursuits such as continuing education and writing "how-to" books. The retiree who seemed least interested in impressing people said: "My only hobby is sleeping late, reading the entire newspaper, and then lying down for a midmorning nap. But other days I take it easy." (Jorgen Patsilevas).

6 To be fair, Juliet Schor does address the causes of competitive consumption indirectly in *The Overspent American* (1998, p. 19). "We live with high levels of denial about the connection between our buying habits and the social statements they make." She is aware that the status drive is so deep in our unconscious that we deny its existence while our actions speak volumes. But she doesn't answer the question of why status is so hardwired in our brains despite what it costs us individually and as a society.

or older males not strong enough or aggressive enough to be warriors. A value system developed that held that gatherer work was servile and not a worthy activity for the hunter class. Being part of the hunter/warrior class had distinct advantages: prestige within the tribe and exemption from tedious forms of work. Within the hunter/warrior class, there were levels of prestige based on reputation for cunning and predatory skills. More aggressive tribes found that attacking neighboring tribes not only reduced competition for game but also provided a valuable source of booty, such as skulls for display, female slaves, weapons, and other goods. Initially this booty was seen as trophies from a successful raid by the tribe as a whole.

But later the display of these trophies outside an individual's hut came to have a different purpose: to confer honor on their owner as possessing superior individual skill. Others sought to emulate the most successful by displaying whatever trophies they came to possess. By association, they, too, gained honor.

The display of trophies or wealth went beyond meeting one's consumption needs, because the motivation for display was honor, not survival. In fact, the more the excess, the more the honor. As societies became more civilized and less dependent on hunting and raids, the importance of conspicuous wealth continued and also evolved. In the past, a successful tribesman might have several wives, some from raids. Later he changed by focusing on a principal wife among others, and then a single wife who became the manager of the family's wealth display, especially concerning matters of dress, furnishings, and style. In this way women became important players in the game of conspicuous consumption.

Prestige in the tribe was the carrot, but a bad reputation for failure was the stick in motivating conspicuous consumption. In early societies, failure could mean death by starvation or otherwise. Later, even when even the unsuccessful could survive, they could still suffer greatly.

A certain standard of wealth . . . is a necessary condition of repu-
tability, and anything in excess of the normal amount is meritorious.

The members of society who fall short of this somewhat indefinite, normal degree of prowess or of property suffer in the esteem of their fellow men; and consequently they suffer in their own esteem, since the usual basis of self-respect is the respect accorded by one's neighbors. . . . Apparent exceptions are met with, especially among people with strong religious convictions.

—Thorstein Veblen
Theory of the Leisure Class (1899, p.38)

Reprinted with permission of CartoonStock Ltd. at cartoonstock.com

Many readers are probably unconvinced that status is an important motivator of human behavior. Some may believe that while status may have been important during the "Gilded Age" of Thorstein Veblen or the "corporate man" generation of William Whyte, Americans are much more casual and democratic about status today. And, there are others who believe that, while status may be important to some, it doesn't affect them. I find this belief prevalent among the young. If pressed, though, most would admit that status is important in the corporate workplace, not to mention the military, even today. Employees are still expected to evidence a certain deference to their superiors. If their bosses earned their position through hard work and talent, then this can be a good thing in the workplace. The problem, though, is that success on the job almost invariably leads, eventually, to conspicuous consumption. The person who has worked long hours to get ahead and made sacrifices, perhaps short-changing his or her family life, feels he or she must have something to show for it. What better than acquiring the finer goods of life? Perhaps some might hope to assuage feelings of guilt about their family by letting them share in this cornucopia of goods. Finally, status on the job is a heady thing. It can be irksome to leave the approbation of the office staff at the end of the day and then be treated like a nobody. By purchasing the proper home, automobile, and clothes, the successful executive can provide clues about their true or pretended career position and how they hope to be treated beyond the workplace.

Much of this status drive is unconscious, according to Thorstein Veblen and Juliet Schor. I know in my own case, it was unconscious. As a mid-level executive in a large corporation, it felt natural to buy upscale items as my income rose. I didn't feel that buying these items was self-promotional. But in my mid-40s, something happened to make me conscious of my desire for conspicuous consumption. I happened to find an unusually good deal on a house for my family, mainly because the owner was not using a real estate agent. The house was the cheapest on a wealthy street. After moving, when I casually mentioned to a new acquaintance that I lived on this street, there was often a visible shift in their body language, and they would suddenly become more attentive. I genuinely had not expected this instantaneous status response. But I was aware of it now, and the feeling was very pleasant. Afterwards, I would look for opportunities to re-experience that high. For example, I might be filling out an application for a bank account that, of course, required my address. When I passed the completed form back to the bank officer, I would hope to see that the officer was impressed. If an address could gain me instant respect, what about a Mercedes?

Vance Packard developed a scale to gauge a person's apparent overall status. It was based on several surveys, done by others, on what people looked for in judging the relative status of their contemporaries. Mr. Packard summarized the measures of status into four categories:

1. Occupation and achieved level in that occupation
2. Level of education
3. Level and source of income
4. Location of home

The last category can serve as a measure of the status derived from conspicuous consumption in general. The first three categories of status can have some moderately negative side effects, like elitism and discrimination. Conspicuous consumption, however, has more serious negative side effects for us and our environment. It robs our lives of time and meaning. The last section of this chapter will address how this happens.

If only we could be successful and yet control our consumption. One conclusion that could be taken from the Packard scale is that with enough success in the first three categories, one could still enjoy high overall status in the eyes of others, without getting caught in the acquisitions trap. At one time in New England, there was an old Yankee tradition of valuing privacy about one's wealth, which avoided this trap.

I've laid the blame for overspending on the doorstep of individual status drive. But this psychological drive has some powerful enablers in Washington and on Madison Avenue. Jonathon Rowe[7] explains some of the changes in the way our economy has worked over the past several decades that caused a sea change in the way Washington views personal consumption.

The contrast is most clear when we compare how two former presidents dealt with national emergencies. Franklin D. Roosevelt, during World War II, challenged Americans to economize on spending and to save by buying war bonds. Sacrifice now for a better future was a familiar Puritan ideal. Seventy years later, George W. Bush, during the war on terrorism, exhorted Americans to go to the malls and spend. Saving was no longer patriotic. Spend, even if you had to borrow to do so. Sacrifice could come later. In Roosevelt's day the production sector was the engine of growth. Now, the service sector, especially finance, health care, and advertising, dominates our economy. Household spending is the engine of growth. The problem is that, unlike our forebears, we have gone beyond really needing much of what we are offered. Part of the economy has become, as Jonathan Rowe put it, a kind of "factory of need," propelled by advertising. The process starts at an early age. According to Juliet Schor in *Born to Buy*, "American children view an estimated 40,000 commercials per year." Meanwhile, advances in financial computer technology have greased the path to consumption.

According to the Federal Reserve Bank, 80 million American households hold at least one credit card, and their total average balance is $8,000. The Internet has made buying virtually instantaneous and opened up more time for shopping. According to Rowe, the majority of Web shopping is done from the office. We can now shop 24/7.

John Kenneth Galbraith writes in *The Affluent Society* (1958, 1998 last rev., pp. 145–146) about how we have come to rely on consumer debt to keep the economy's "factory of need" humming.

---

7 "Wasted Time, Wasted Work," *Take Back Your Time* (2003, pp. 58–65), ed. by John de Graaf.

Advertising and emulation, the two dependent sources of desire, work across society. They operate on those who can afford and those who cannot. With those who lack the current means, it is a brief and obvious step from stimulating their desire by advertising to making it effective in the market with a loan. . . . The process of persuading people to incur debt, and the arrangements for them to do so, are as much a part of modern production as the making of the goods and the nurturing of the wants. The Puritan ethos [save for the future] was not abandoned. It was merely overwhelmed by the massive power of modern merchandising.

Galbraith goes on to point out that large consumer debt has added a significant new risk that could increase the magnitude of future recessions. His predictions came true in spectacular form during the Great Recession of 2007–2009.[8] Consumer debt creation has become a major accelerant, expanding and adding to demand when the economy is booming, contracting and accelerating the decline in consumer spending during recessions.

A numerical example may help illustrate how consumer debt can worsen a recession. John Doe earns $80,000 a year. His house's value has appreciated well in the housing boom. Advertising convinces him to tap his new wealth through home equity loans. Over the next few years he is able to increase his spending by $10,000 a year to $90,000 while rolling the 5 percent interest expense back into the loan. The home equity loans build to $100,000, lowering his remaining equity. Then the impossible happens. A recession begins, and home values actually decline. His home equity disappears, and all further borrowing is cut off. Not only does his lifestyle have to drop by the $10,000 per year that he can no longer borrow, but also the $5,000 in interest expense he is forced to start repaying. His lifestyle drops from $90,000 a year to $75,000. Ouch!

---

8 John Kenneth Galbraith died in 2006 and didn't live to see The Great Recession of 2007–09 in which consumer debt played an unprecedented negative role.

Talking about an individual's drive for status compared to the past, for example, to his or her parents, can be disheartening. Remember that today's Joneses are richer than the Joneses our parents faced. Let's assume someone had upper-middle-class parents who had worked hard and surpassed the Joneses of their day, and that they received a certain level of satisfaction or utility from that. Their children also work hard and surpass the Joneses of their day. Despite much higher income than their parents, however, their satisfaction would be no greater, because they reached only the same relative level of status. But the children must pay a higher personal price because of greater negative side effects. To match the Joneses of today, the children must worker longer hours. Their mother may not have worked at all. And, because of less free time and more clutter from overconsumption, they experience more stress. Also, they're probably fatter from relying more on timesaving convenience foods. The squeeze on free time from higher income is addressed in the next section.

OF INCOME AND TIME

> Even in the cities people are called "Englishmen" when they turn
> up on the dot at meetings or appointments.
>
> —Margaret Mead
>
> *Cultural Patterns and Technical Change* (1953, p. 90)
>
> [She is referring to the casual attitude toward time she found in Greece.]

According to Swedish economist Dr. Staffan B. Linder,[9] mainstream economists have not taken full account of time constraints in analyzing consumer behavior, and they have been ignoring its noneconomic impact on quality of life. Mainstream economists do treat time at work as a limited resource, but only work time. Consumption, by implication, is instantaneous, and other uses of

---

9 Staffan B. Linder, *The Harried Leisure Class*, 1970.

time are unlimited and free, like air and water. Yet, people in wealthy countries are continually complaining about the absence of free time and the resulting stress. In addition, when offered a choice between using their productivity gains for more free time or for more hours of work, workers will oddly choose more work, even when their basic consumer needs are fully met. Economists have been at a loss to explain this choice, which doesn't fit their theories of marginal utility and substitution. Dr. Linder tries to address this paradox by pointing out that consumption, far from being instantaneous, consumes a great deal of time. As acquisitions become extensive, we need not only a lot of time to shop for and enjoy them, but we need additional time for their upkeep, leaving much less free time in our week compared to our less-affluent past.

Dr. Linder uses economic analysis, including the usual overly simplified economist's assumptions, to demonstrate what would happen in an environment where highly specialized workmen with superior hourly income continued to experience even more growth in income. Their already high commitment of time to consumption and maintenance of their extensive acquisitions would force them to hire others to help with the upkeep of their property. To pay for this the worker would substitute longer factory or office hours for fewer hours of maintenance work at home. As long as they were earning more in their specialty than the hired service people, this could make economic sense. Historically, economic growth has always been accompanied by a rising share of the service sector compared to the production sector. So, higher hourly income can increase, not decrease, the desire for work time, even for those already well off. Dr. Linder felt that the utility value of free-time activities would not keep pace with the utility of work and consumption time for workers earning a high income, say $50 an hour, because it would not be possible to significantly leverage the enjoyment of free time with additional consumer goods. Cultural activities can cost very little, but less intellectual pursuits, such as watching giant screen televisions or driving expensive cars, can provide entertainment while doing double duty in building status through conspicuous consumption.

[E]conomic growth subjects culture time to an increasing competition, and the time devoted to cultural exercise is probably decreas-
ing. . . . We have long expressed hope that the elimination of material
cares would clear the way for a broad cultural advancement. In practice,
not even those endowed with the necessary intellectual and emotional
capacity have shown any propensity for immersing themselves in the
cultivation of their minds and spirit. The tendency is rather the reverse.

—Staffan B. Linder
The Harried Leisure Class (1970, pp. 2 & 94)

Economists had thought higher income would cause workers to prefer
more free time because of the effect of declining marginal utility on consumption. That theory had helped to explain behavior in other situations. After
all, the marginal utility or satisfaction of eating the fifth hamburger in a row
is obviously less than for the first one. If consumption were mainly for basic
food and shelter, one might eventually reach saturation.[10] Then, more free
time for cultural activities would seem attractive. But, for the affluent, most
consumption is honorific or purposely conspicuous. The more you spend on
these goods, the greater your status. And, status has no diminishing marginal
utility; there is virtually infinite potential satisfaction. Therefore, consumption is limited only by an individual's income and the time to spend it all.
"Expenditures rise to meet income," is a Parkinson's Law. Because of all the
time high-magnitude consumption takes, we have, in my opinion, a truism:
More income means less free time.

---

10   According to John Kenneth Galbraith in *The Affluent Society* (1958, p. 121), conventional economists incorrectly accounted for the continuation of high marginal utility
for consumption—even after basic needs are met—on the greater variety of choices that
open up to the consumer as his or her income rises. Dr. Galbraith quotes one of these
conventional economists: "Today, after a large increase in his income, he has extended his
consumption to include cable television and eccentric loafers. . . . Things have changed;
he is a different man; there is no real standard for comparison." Dr. Galbraith did not
agree with this analysis.

Of course, it may be hard to believe that consumption takes significant time.[11] One reason is that the time element in consumption can seem trivial since people usually enjoy shopping for and using their purchases, and so there is not much awareness of time loss. A personal reality check can be useful. Reconnoiter and take a rough inventory of your closets, attic, basement, and garage. Every item in there was probably a must-have in its day. Recall the history of a few of the items: the researching, the shopping, the various occasions of use, and the upkeep and storage. Imagine multiplying that by thousands, and you may have a new sense of the time spent in consumption of goods. And, don't forget the uncounted items that go out every week in the trash.

Some of our actions are giveaways that we intuitively know there is limited time to consume all the goods we can afford. One coping strategy is not just to buy goods faster but also to buy more expensive ones. In this way one gains more satisfaction and status in the same amount of time. Thorstein Veblen noted how handcrafted items were often preferred over mass-produced ones, even when they were more expensive and less utilitarian. Another time-saver is multitasking, such as watching television while eating dinner or talking on the cell phone while walking the dog. Saving time by paying others to maintain our property was mentioned above. The ultimate consumption timesaver, though, is simply to store or discard our acquisitions even while they are still useful. It saves maintenance time and opens up the opportunity to purchase new objects that can further boost one's satisfaction.

---

11   Ironically, we see most of our major purchases as time savers. Driving a car certainly saves time over the alternative of walking. And, most adult Americans, outside major mass transit areas, don't really have any alternative to driving. Robert Bernstein in *Take Back Your Time* (p. 103) estimates that it takes two minutes to earn enough to drive a mile, based on average wages of $15 per hour and data from AAA showing that the owning and operating cost for an average car is around 50¢ per mile. With typical miles driven per car per year of 12,000, he calculates that the average motorist spends 850 hours per year either driving the car or earning the money to pay for it. The convenience of a car is obvious. The hidden cost is the commitment of time implicit in the decision to own one. This is time that will no longer be available for other choices. If time were infinite in our lives, there would be no problem.

"It cost $699. But when you factor in the time wasted sitting in front of it, well, the real cost is enormous."

Growth in consumer spending has become the overarching goal of American economic policy. The current elevated level is sustained by heroic stimulation of demand for goods that were unnecessary the year before. In the past, in a world of scarcity, an individual's failure to work and spend was considered injurious to the general welfare. But, in a world of affluence, where is the injury of an individual not working or spending to his or her maximum?

Anthropologists, like Margaret Mead, have been struck by the different concepts of time that exist in other cultures. (Her quote appears at the beginning of this section.) It is almost as if these other concepts of time were hatched on a different planet, suggesting that our own concept may not be as absolute as we thought. You can find these strange concepts in cultures that have a time surplus resulting from low economic activity.

> [T]he Nuer have no expression equivalent to time in our language, and they cannot, therefore, as we can, speak of time as though it were something actual, which passes, can be wasted, can be saved and so forth. I do not think that they ever experienced the same feeling of fighting against time or having to coordinate their activities with an abstract passage of time, because their points of reference are mainly the activities themselves, which are generally of a leisurely character. Events follow a logical order, but they are not controlled by an abstract system. . . . Nuer are fortunate."
>
> —Edward T. Hall, *The Silent Language* (1959, Ch. 9)
> [The Nuer were a pastoral people living in the Sudan.]

By contrast we know we live in a time-starved culture by the importance we give to time. As Linder summarizes (pp. 22–23):

> What has happened is that in rich countries all slacks in the use of time have been eliminated, so far as humanly possible. The attitude to time is dictated entirely by the commodity's extreme scarcity. . . . The pocket calendar became our most important book. Its loss causes the owner himself to feel lost. Punctuality has become a virtue we demand of those around us. Waiting is a squandering of time that angers people in rich countries. Only personal mismanagement or the inconsiderate behavior of others will create brief—and highly irritating—periods of involuntary idleness. . . . This tyranny [of the clock] has developed, step by step, with our successful revolution against the dictatorship of material poverty.

CHAPTER TWO

RETIREMENT, INVESTING AND TAMING STATUS

THERE WAS A TIME NOT LONG AGO

A few short decades ago, retirement plans were simply called pensions. Where I worked in Hartford, Connecticut, home of several insurance giants, pension and Social Security benefits for a retired career employee could provide lifetime income close to what they earned in their final years of work. And these pensions often included future inflation protection.

This era of generous benefits spawned an unusual group of private organizations made up of retired male executives. The first in Hartford, founded in 1970, was called the Old Guard. These clubs blossomed all across the country because, back then, retirement was seen as a time in life to explore alternatives to work. The Old Guard met weekly to listen and learn from guest speakers. Members could choose from a variety of club-sponsored sports leagues for golf, bowling, and so on. Excursions to local attractions with wives included were offered throughout the year. Even group trips to Europe were arranged for interested members. A retiree could potentially fill a large part of his week with club activities, especially if he also volunteered for club office or for sponsored charitable activities.

In the beginning, the Old Guard carried a certain exclusivity. Members typically came from the executive ranks of major Hartford institutions. The demand for membership was so great that a waiting list developed, and two new clubs were spun off. I joined one of the spin-offs, The Squires, in 2008. In the next seven years, its membership dropped from 120 to 80. Members reminisce about the days when the club numbered more than 350. The reason for this dramatic decline is obvious. Men of normal retirement age in their sixties are no longer looking for alternatives to work. Typical new members are now in their mid-seventies.

The day of the traditional pension and of retirement clubs has passed. This is the 401(k) era, since the time corporations decided to turn most of the risk of funding retirement over to their employees. Work has clawed its way into the retirement years.

Any day of the week, we can find articles about our woefully inadequate 401(k) balances. Retirement planning has become big business at our major financial institutions. The advice is boringly similar: work longer and sign up for a professional plan. Some writers even rationalize that working longer is better for you anyway, psychologically.[12] Implicit is the message that there are no known alternative lifestyles superior to work. But the existence of retirement clubs, like the Old Guard and The Squires, is evidence that, at one time, retirees felt differently.

12　"Whatever the motivation, it's clear that the old model of retirement . . .is thankfully on its way to being retired. Research from the Transamerica Center for Retirement Studies found that two-thirds of baby boomers plan to work past age 65 or not retire at all . . .. In fact, those who extend their years in the work world . . . are more satisfied with life and have better mental well-being, less depression and higher cognitive performance, according to research [not identified]." www.marketwatch.com/story/retirement-is-bad-for-your-health-and-your-wealth-2014–06–20?dist=countdown

PREPARING FOR LEISURE

"It's easy to become a Buddhist after you've made your first million."

—Eric Rosenbaum

The Street, March 15, 2012

www.thestreet.com

We have been talking about the trade-off between work and leisure. Leisure is generally misunderstood and thought to be any time left over after work, or free time. Currently, in our society, the chief purposes of free time are first to renew ourselves for tomorrow's work, and second, to use it in ways that promote our status. In other times and other societies, leisure was seen as an important opportunity to pursue culture and the meaning of life.

Throwbacks like me, who find cultural leisure attractive, need to recognize the obstacles we face. Otherwise, we may find ourselves wondering later how so many years have slipped by with no serious attempt to engage in cultural leisure. The main obstacle is an inborn and insatiable desire for conspicuous consumption facilitated by propaganda from commercial institutions that whip up this desire on a daily basis. Consuming for status is the juice that moves our economy, but it is addictive and destructive to leisure time.

The current career outlook for many is a time trap with dubious spiritual meaning. Those who view this effort negatively call it a rat race. Of course, many, if not most Americans, have too little income or too much responsibility to do anything other than to continue spending the most they can. For centuries, though, a few have experimented with alternative less-materialistic lifestyles outside of religion. Historical examples of group efforts include: Bohemian communities, communes, utopian societies like Brook Farm and New Harmony, as well as religious or cult settlements. But, basically, the conclusion of the history I see is that these efforts don't last. Less documented are individual experiments. Some examples of people who tried to escape the rat race alone, and without independent wealth, are mentioned in this book. My belief, based on observation of a few former financial planning clients who tried to escape is that the vast majority will later return to the rat race.

The struggle to dematerialize our lives by dropping out is ultimately a struggle with ourselves. In truth, we want the same things as others in our society, and that includes status and respect; so dropping out goes against our own nature. Even those lucky few who inherit enough to live without work can't avoid the respect issue. Society understands and respects not working in only one situation: if you can call it retirement, not counting disability or stay-at-home parenting. However, traditional retirement is wasted on the old. By the time we reach retirement age, we may have the money, but not the energy to pursue leisure, and by then we will have been brainwashed on the joys of work and consumption for sixty-plus years.

A footnote in the first chapter refers to a survey of several dozen people who were qualified for or in retirement. A survey like this can provide a window into how one group of older people responded to the reality of finally not having to work. For the vast majority, the number-one activity in retirement was work, either full time, part time, or work in some new form. Teresa Ghilarducci in her book *When I'm Sixty-Four* (2008, p. 3), noticed the same inability of the "retired" to find meaning outside of work: "However, all people seem defensive about the notion of retirement, quickly asserting that 'they wanted to be productive, not shrivel up and die.'" In other words, by age sixty-five, many Americans cannot conceive of any *meaningful* alternative to work, other than death. If we don't want to end up like that, it's probably not a good idea to wait until sixty-five to start learning about cultural leisure.

> The enjoyment of cultural and other pleasures of the mind, in particular, does not come easily. A person must be trained. It is work, though not of the physical sort. . . . Our society has failed to provide

the requisite education, which is why so many people get their enjoyment from the modern version of Roman circuses, our television programs and sports.

—Joseph E. Stiglitz (Nobel Prize economist)
"Toward a General Theory of Consumerism"
Revisiting Keynes (2010, p.57)
Ed. by Lorenzo Pecchi and Gustavo Piga

I tried for years to pursue my vague desire for cultural leisure while still working. But, there never seemed to be time to focus in on exactly what I was looking for. I suspected then, and now believe fully, that the time needed to achieve this focus will be found only in full retirement. My attempts did produce two benefits, though. First, I learned about the obstacles to cultural leisure; and second, I learned to devise financial plans for achieving retirement, which I secretly hoped would be an early retirement.

Part of these plans was my concept of "owning your job," as an interim financial stage before retirement. For this, you may need the help of a financial planner to do some of the calculations. The goal is to put on paper the financial conditions under which you could afford to stop working for, say, two years, by building a kind of super emergency fund, while staying on track with other saving goals, such as your children's college education and a normal retirement. This doesn't mean you would quit when you reach that goal. That's why I call it "owning your job." But, the peace of mind of knowing that you are not necessarily trapped in your current job is very gratifying, especially if job burnout starts creeping in during mid-to-late career. You might still be in the rat race, but it could help to know you are there voluntarily for now. Then, if your current job becomes intolerable, you have the savings backstop, not just to look for work in the same field but possibly to be retrained in a new field that may pay less but brings more meaning.

In addition, once you "own your job," self-employment and entrepreneurship are more realistic alternatives, because they are less threatening to your family's financial security. If you reach this stage early in life and then continue to save for more years, early retirement, too, becomes a possibility. In summary, the key benefit of job ownership is flexibility: flexibility to adjust financially to unforeseeable opportunities such as entrepreneurship or a voluntary early retirement offer from your employer, or to unforeseen difficulties like layoffs and mandatory early retirement. Finally, the process of documenting your financial goals and understanding their potentially positive results can motivate you to learn about the obstacles, such as conspicuous consumption, that stand in your way. Budgeting and other abilities that you acquire in gaining control of your financial lifestyle will bring the day of full financial freedom much closer, especially if you learn how to live on less.

One way to approach this is first to map out the year-by-year savings trajectory you would need to be on to be able to put your children through college and to retire at age sixty-five. Then superimpose a target of additional savings, equivalent to two years of your current earned income, to be reached at a target age before sixty-five. That target age could be after your children finish college. Saving 10 percent of your earned income is typically seen as good. You might have to go well beyond that, which is why you'll eventually have to address your approach to status spending. We'll take a closer look at taming the status beast further on. From time to time you'll need to revise your plan to take into account an expanding family, job changes, and other unforeseen challenges.

The New York Times (September 15, 2012) had some crude, but useful, rules of thumb from Fidelity Investments. Starting with assumptions of $100,000 in living expenses at age sixty-seven *and full Social Security benefits*, Fidelity Investments estimates, for plain-vanilla, one-person retirement, you would need to have $800,000 saved in a 401(k), IRA, and other marketable securities, or eight times expenses. To be on track earlier in your career, you should be at three times current expenses by age forty-five, and five times by age fifty-five. To fit this with the concept of "owning our job" by, say, age fifty at an expense level of $75,000, you would need six times (4+2), or $450,000, plus enough to cover any remaining child college expenses. At that level of savings, you would be ahead of schedule by two extra years and could be said to "own your job." One last point here. The $75,000 in this example refers to expenses, not necessarily to earned income. If you could permanently reduce spending 20 percent by downsizing your lifestyle, to $60,000 in annual expenses, you would need only $360,000 in savings to "own your job."

Continuing this simplistic example a bit further, we could try to roughly estimate the cost of voluntary early retirement. You need to calculate how much additional savings would be needed to cover expenses, this time with no current help from Social Security or health insurance, for the retirement years prior to age sixty-seven and still be left with $800,000 at sixty-seven. You definitely should have professional financial help before seriously considering this option. However, for speculative purposes in this example, you could add $100,000 for every year before sixty-seven. Say then, at age sixty you would need $1,500,000 to have $800,000 left at sixty-seven. Realistically then, your superior earning power and disciplined financial lifestyle would need to be heroic, but not impossible.

Reaching job ownership before retirement age will pivot on success in your career while, at the same time, avoiding for decades the pitfalls of conspicuous consumption. We're talking about, for example, maintaining a *middle* middle-class lifestyle while earning an *upper* middle-class income. It's quite a psychological challenge to spend below your income class. Imagine watching an old friend, earning about the same as you, parking his new Lexus SUV next to your old Subaru in the driveway of your middling starter home, and then hearing your spouse and children squeal with delight at the sight of his car.

It is important to be clear that achieving job ownership depends on having a successful career, *not* on successful investing, while keeping firm controls on spending. Wall Street thrives on convincing people that their vaunted expertise will help make us richer sooner, and human greed makes us want to believe them. I've witnessed more cases than I like to remember in which grand investment schemes and high fees torpedoed a worker's savings. The analogy may not be entirely fair, but I am reminded of the comment made concerning the eye-popping casino towers in Las Vegas and Connecticut: *They weren't built with the owner's money but with the losers' money.* You don't want to be funding Wall Street's towers. This doesn't mean that it is impossible to find a trustworthy financial adviser who can help, but the emphasis should be on keeping you out of trouble, not reaching for too-good-to-be-true returns. Career and saving habits are the real engines of growth in wealth. The main investment goal should be to prevent inflation and taxes from overly deflating savings.

A career in religion is a socially acceptable way to reduce the need for materialistic status and, perhaps, to fit in time for reflection and contemplation. If this career path doesn't appeal to you, then you're probably going to have to come to terms with the time and cost of exhibiting status in contemporary America. I, personally, haven't found it possible to pursue career and true cultural leisure simultaneously. As pointed out previously, work and cultural leisure are *opposites*, like trying to serve two masters. Of course, you can dabble, but I believe the main attraction of finding moments of transcendence is available on a regular basis only when leisure is the master, which may not be possible until one has retired.

In the meantime, though, one can try to maintain a taste for culture by reading philosophy and other subjects in the liberal arts. Courses offered by The Teaching Company, which sometimes can be found free at the library, and similar online courses offered by individual colleges, are attractive ways to hear college professors teach these subjects. For meditation, look for a local group that meets regularly for *zazen* practice. These are just a few examples among many possibilities. I hope it's self-evident that this is cheap entertainment. Strangely, there seems to be an inverse relationship between the quality of cultural leisure and its cost. People often confuse leisure with costly recreation. One reason people don't want more time off work is that many free-time activities, like travel, golf, and entertaining, can be expensive. If time off were more rewarding and inexpensive, we might feel differently.

At this point, it is probably important to add balance to this discussion of work. Otherwise, it may sound as though work is some kind of purgatory one must go through to reach the heaven of leisure. Perhaps in Aristotle's day, it was possible to balance work and leisure harmoniously while still young. Contemporary society, however, puts the emphasis on work first, then leisure. Work is a fact of life, and without it, leisure is not possible financially and probably not possible psychologically, either. The latter point is brought home for me by the acquaintances I have known who inherited large wealth but did not have the slightest interest in contemplative leisure. Instead, they had the dubious distinction of pursuing conspicuous consumption without the supposed justification of having earned it.[13]

Karl Marx believed that esoteric pursuits like cultural leisure were elitist activities and that the real meaning of life was found in action, not thought. The highest form of life for Marx was self-directed work that effectively utilized one's special talents in a world in which one had control of their work and time. I believe that most American economists, if pressed, would agree with Marx that self-directed and meaningful work is a worthy goal in capitalist economies as well as in communist economies.

---

13 The less favorable view of inherited wealth may be a recent phenomenon. Not too many years ago—say in Vance Packard's day—inherited wealth was seen as superior, status-wise, to earned wealth. Old money was viewed as more prestigious, which, in turn, may have been a holdover from a time when the ideas of inherited aristocracy held more sway. I believe, though, that in my lifetime, earned wealth has surpassed inherited wealth as a marker of meritorious accomplishment in America.

The American psychologist Abraham Maslow coined "self-actualization" and John Rawls the term "self-realization" to refer to a person's
emerging mastery and unfolding scope. . . . These two Americans
understood that most, if not all, of the attainable self-realization in
modern societies can come only from a career. We cannot all go
tilting at windmills, but we can take on the challenges of career. If
a challenging career is not the main hope for self-realization, what
else could be?

—Edmund S. Phelps

"Corporations and Keynes"

Revisiting Keynes (2010, p. 101)

Ed. by Lorenzo Pecchi & Gustavo Piga

Work does offer psychological benefits aside from status, especially if it's
self-directed and meaningful. Marx believed that this was not possible in
capitalist countries, where the owners of capital make the decisions about how
and when workers work. But capitalist countries have evolved to include labor
unions and governmental oversight to give workers some say, in a general sense,
in how their work is structured. In large corporations and partnerships, however, to reach a level of control that allows a high degree of self-actualization,
one needs to rise fairly high in the organization. The odds are not good, given
the large number of competitors for the few top positions. Capitalism is at its
best in its encouragement of entrepreneurship, and in my opinion, this is the
path that offers the best chance, along with self-employment, of reaching the
pinnacle of self-actualization in a career.

A career as a path to self-actualization can indeed bring happiness and
meaning to life as well as provide status and a secure retirement. So, we should
make the most of it. I just happen to believe that leisure, when you can afford
it, can provide even more happiness and meaning. Abraham Maslow, the father

of career self-actualization, referred to an even higher state of being he called "peak-experiences," that typically are unrelated to one's career. So, the path forward is to achieve in work while saving for a future transition to leisure. Then, achieve even greater happiness in leisure.

INVESTING

An individual or couple planning for a normal or early retirement would need to build substantial savings to support twenty-five to thirty years of not working. In this chapter I made suggestions about how to build those savings, mainly by avoiding the conspicuous consumption trap, with only brief mention of investing. As a former professional investment manager, it's difficult for me to open this subject and limit my comments to less than a book. There are already plenty of those books. I'll keep it brief.

The financial markets will provide a fair return over the long run, if you're careful. If a fair return is not good enough, and you become greedy, you will be burned. Your best friend is long-term compound interest, and your major ally is diversification. But in order for compound interest to make a meaningful contribution, your savings need to reach a critical mass well before retirement.

Here's an example. Let's assume that age fifty is the key year for critical mass. With good compounding of returns and continuing yearly contributions, your savings at age fifty could triple, possibly quadruple, by age sixty-five to sixty-seven. $200,000 at age fifty would probably not provide the critical mass, even with another fifteen years of compounding, to fund a twenty-five to thirty-year retirement. But $300,000 might be enough.

If compound interest and diversification are your friends, then greed, ignorance, and investment fees are your enemies. John Bogle of the Vanguard Funds tells us that in his experience with 401(k) retirement and IRA accounts, savers lose more than one-third of their potential returns to investment fees.[14] This loss compromises the savers' probability of reaching critical mass by age fifty. But, how does the saver, with limited investment expertise, achieve a fair market return without losing a third of it in fees to professional managers?

I would like to see a requirement that—to qualify for tax advantages, employers would have to offer a low-cost *standard* option in the menu of investment choices available to employees in their 401(k) plans. The cost of this option would be kept to a minimum through the use of indexed investments. The makeup of the investment portfolio in the standard option could be designed by a government entity or by a panel of recognized experts from outside Wall Street, perhaps from academia. The employee's choice to use the standard option would be voluntary. The mechanics become more complicated when we begin to speculate on where the funds would be held. But an official standard option has no chance of adoption, because of investment industry opposition. So, let's focus on the concept rather than implementation details.

A standard investment option would hopefully be very low cost and offer a virtual certainty of a fair return at the lowest possible risk, relative to the returns and risks inherent in the overall financial markets. Also hopefully, it could be executable by anyone with typical investment knowledge. My image of this option would be a portfolio with a 60 percent commitment

---

14   See interview of John Bogle on *Frontline*, a PBS news series, April 23, 2013. Actually, he said that over a 50-year investing lifetime—including the years in retirement—investment fees can erode *63 percent* of what an investor could have earned because of "the tyranny of compounding costs." My estimate of one-third erosion refers only to the twenty-five to thirty-year accumulation period. *Consumer Reports* echoes Bogle in their review titled "Stop 401(k) Fees from Cheating You out of Retirement Money" (August 2013). "You might think the most important element in picking a mutual fund in a 401(k) is past performance or the experience of the fund's manager. But the best predictor of a fund's performance is fees, says the investment research company Morningstar. No matter what type of fund: large-cap, small-cap, value or growth—lower fees correlate with better performance. That's because although stocks go up and down, fees are a constant. Over the long haul, higher fees drag down a fund's overall return."

to a well-diversified stock index fund and 40 percent committed to a well-diversified bond index fund.[15]

The 40 percent committed to fixed income could include money market funds as an emergency reserve, but that would be limited to 10 percent overall. The beauty of this portfolio is that it would require no ongoing management, with one exception. The 60/40 mix and the 10 percent money market limit would need to be maintained over time. So, at least annually, the portfolio should be *rebalanced,* selling some of the winning asset class and buying some of the losing asset class to keep the ratio at 60/40. This helps to offset the effects of one asset class becoming overly inflated and prone to a large correction. There would be at least two additional versions of the basic portfolio; an aggressive version for investors with high risk tolerance and/or under age forty could simply employ a 70/30 mix. The conservative version for those with low risk tolerance and/or over age fifty would use a 50/50 mix. (In footnote 15 I approximate how one could replicate a "standard" mix in a non-401(k) account, like an IRA.)

Most employer 401(k) plans do not offer the specific mutual funds listed in footnote 15 but may offer index funds that are similar. The challenge will be, for those investors who like the idea of an idiot-proof standard option, to try to find the closest index mutual fund substitutes and then combine the choices for the target 60/40 mix. Of course, in a personal IRA or taxable account, one could invest in the actual Vanguard mutual funds and hold (or put in custody) the funds at Vanguard itself to avoid unrequested,

---

15 For example, an individual trying to create his or her own "standard option" could put their 60 percent stock commitment in the Vanguard Total Stock Market Index Fund Admiral Shares (VTSAX) and their 40 percent bond commitment in the Vanguard Total Bond Market Index Fund Admiral Shares (VBTLX). The fees currently for these funds are 0.05 percent and 0.10 percent, respectively. The stock fund holds about 3,500 stocks, and the bond fund, about 6,000 bonds. Hence, diversification is quite extensive, and a market return is assured. The investments could be held at Vanguard, and if a money market fund is needed, their Prime Money Market Fund (VMMXX)—the largest U.S. money market fund—could be used. I must point out that this discussion of mutual funds is for example, not actual advice.

and sometimes tempting, investment advice that may result if held at other institutions.

If you chose a standard investment option approach, you probably want to keep it to yourself. Sharing it with others may open you to derision, especially from those who feel they are experts. You will have the last laugh. We have just seen that by using paid advisers, retirement savers may forfeit a third of the return provided by the markets. The standard option described here is designed to make sure that doesn't happen. The real human problem, though, is that index fund investing, just like saving, is boring, and discussion of active investing, especially in individual companies, makes for interesting small talk at cocktail parties. Bragging about investment successes (while ignoring inconvenient losses) can become another way to promote status.

We've mentioned using a financial planner on occasion. Not long ago, there was a clear distinction between professionals calling themselves investment advisers or brokers and those calling themselves financial planners. But each has seen advantages in the other's business model, and they've tried to combine the most useful features of both. So investment advisers now offer financial planning because of its strong marketing appeal, while financial planners offer investment management for its steady compensation.

It no longer matters much what advisers calls themselves; they usually share the same business model. That model focuses on bringing accounts in-house under asset management agreements, while first offering written plans as a lead into investment management, similar to a loss leader in retail. The beauty for the adviser of having assets under management is that it provides regular, predictable compensation, and the fees can be deducted directly from the accounts quarterly. In other words, advisers don't have to ask the client for a check every time they are compensated. A stand-alone written financial plan, however, will probably require that the prospect write a check. And for a comprehensive and truly customized plan, that check can be several thousand dollars.

Whereas investment management may cost more in fees than it's worth, the value of an unbiased financial plan from an independent planner is usually worth *more* than it costs. For one thing, the written advice would cover more than investing and offer ways to save money in other financial areas such as taxes, insurance, and budgeting. You can see the challenge, though. Planners often operate under a conflict of interest. They know that corralling of investment assets in-house is the best path to business success, and yet they're expected to keep this fact from unconsciously influencing the plan they produce.

The only advice I can give is to clarify up front that the planner or the firm will not be managing your assets but that you're willing to pay a fair price for the planner's time in writing the plan. Perhaps it will also prove useful to pay for a review of the plan after a year or two, but the assets would remain under the client's management, thereby saving investment fees. This should be feasible if the plan is thorough and uses index funds. The best place to start looking for a planner, with proven expertise in writing comprehensive plans, is the National Association of Fee-Only Financial Planners (NAPFA, www. napfa.org). Members' credentials go well beyond the basic Certified Financial Planner (CFP) designation.

Assuming you are able to obtain a thorough financial plan paying an hourly or fixed fee, you will still need to implement the investment portion of the plan. Previously, your choices were to do it yourself or sign an investment management contract with a local investment adviser. This latter choice, though, with its automatic quarterly fee, exacerbated the challenge of controlling costs. The Vanguard Group, which revolutionized the mutual fund industry with low-cost index funds for individuals, is now trying to do the same with low cost portfolio management. Charles Schwab and others are joining the effort. These services are called "robo-advisers," implying a degree of automation to lower costs. (Vanguard insists their service is a hybrid, providing telephone and email contact with an investment professional.) Compared to the typical

1% fee charged by local professionals, Vanguard charges 0.3% and has low cost access to their stable of industry-leading index funds and ETFs. Although starting late, Vanguard has jumped to an early lead with $47 billion in robo-adviser assets at the end of 2016. Charles Schwab is second with $12.3 billion. For accounts of $50,000 or more, this approach provides a viable middle road between do-it-yourself and the 1% fee world of local investment advisers.

TAMING STATUS

As we've seen, if you want true cultural leisure in retirement, you need to be prepared to sacrifice some status. As income grows, leisure time theoretically becomes more affordable. But, status improvements also become more affordable. Status is instinctual and widely accepted socially, and therefore usually wins the battle, resulting in more spending and less free time. Thus, rising income actually pushes leisure further away, and this has been our history.

In my experience, young adults are convinced that status does not affect their spending decisions. And that's how I remember myself at that age as well. Other than as an academic interest—say like reading *The Status Seekers*—status did not reach my conscious awareness as a personal experience until I was in my forties, when my income had finally reached a critical mass so that I could make purchases that immediately elevated my status. Looking back, though, I see I'd been making purchases all along that had been based on unconscious status motivations.

One hard-not-to-notice status purchase is a luxury automobile. When I see a Lexus or a Mercedes, I assume they have middle-aged owners who have achieved a level of affluence. To me, the owners came to a fork and took the wrong road, in which more spending beat out more saving. Unless they are one of the exceptionally wealthy, I can see them at a future point past their peak earning years, living with only a thin financial cushion and lacking flexibility to meet unexpected difficulties or opportunities, and having to work well into their retirement years. And, it didn't have to be that way, because once they had excess income to save. But they chose the status road.

To tame status, we need to be consciously aware of its effects. A good place to start is acknowledging that that advertising really does affect us. To believe otherwise defies logic. Can we truly believe that profit-maximizing American business owners would spend $280 billion a year on advertising, and not expect it to produce far more in sales? Think about that when you're in your car driving to the mall to buy that great outfit you saw on TV before the sale ends.

Advertising no longer pretends to be informative. It is filled with rapid flashes of thin, attractive people doing cool things with a sexy voice-over informing us how much better life would be if we just buy this product. The ad may seem silly when you watch, but it works, because we don't have to be paying attention for it to work. Perhaps we would be better off paying attention to what advertisements are suggesting and deciding consciously whether that's what we really want to buy.

Advertisers often appeal directly to our desire for status in an ad for a major purchase, like a luxury car or posh housing development. But more subtle advertising appeals to our sense of taste or style, which is based on our unconscious beliefs about class distinctions. Just as Thorstein Veblen brought conspicuous consumption into our awareness, Pierre Bourdieu brought taste affectations into our awareness. His book, *A Social Critique of the Judgment of Taste* (1984), was a well-documented analysis of the correlations between perceived class identity and the consumption patterns of French society in the 1960s and 1970s. According to Juliet Schor, Bourdieu used his subjects' educational attainment and father's occupation as a proxy for their class affiliation. What he documented was a high statistical correlation between a person's class and their taste.

For example, in classical music, the lower-class subject could confidently be predicted to prefer the light classics such as the "Blue Danube Waltz," while the upper class preferred complex classics, like a Bach fugue. The lower class invariably bought their furniture in department stores, while the rich leisurely perused the antique shops. The middle class, not surprisingly, fell in between but emulated the upper class by buying knockoffs of expensive items. Bourdieu concluded that, while we think our taste in which item or service to buy is just based randomly on who we are, in reality it's heavily influenced by our unconscious desire to project a certain class identification.

"Elegance is an attitude"

Many would dispute how much spending is driven by perceived class identifications, but I believe it is a significant element in conspicuous consumption. In the blunt form of conspicuous consumption, you might build a McMansion, a mansion-size home on postage-stamp lot designed to produce brute shock and awe, rather than to convey one's good taste. A subtle taste display, though, could be achieved, as in the famous Vance Packard example, by first finding a couple of old portraits in an antique store of a man and a woman, and then hanging the portraits in the dining room, hoping guests will assume they are your ancestors. It would convey the impression of a long and proud family history.

The difficulty is that purchases designed to demonstrate taste are invariably more expensive than the plain-vanilla versions. That's part of their mystique and the role they play in conspicuous consumption. Advertisers and salespeople will appeal to your preferred class identification with the suggestion that the right kind of people always prefer quality over cost. But if you're trying to tame your status-based consumption, it's important to be aware of the role taste affectations play in driving spending decisions. Unfortunately, curtailing this type of spending can cut deeply into one's sense of identity, and this consequence should not be underestimated.

> To maintain psychological comfort, most of us must transcend the strictures of the current consumption map. We must go "beyond Bourdieu," if you will. The first step is to decouple spending from our sense of personal worth, a connection basic to all hierarchical consumption maps. The second is to find a reference group for whom a low-cost lifestyle is socially acceptable.
>
> —Juliet B. Schor
> *The Overspent American* (1998, p. 139)

Juliet Schor is suggesting that our current status spending is driven by a deep need for personal identity and social acceptance, which unconsciously translates into a consumption map. To try to alter this map with arbitrary cuts may result in psychological distress. We can transcend our current map, though, by developing an authentic self-identity that questions the link between our self-worth and what we own. What might also help is keeping our eyes on the prize of the future payoff we could receive from the buildup of substantial savings, as described above. I also believe meditation, over time, results in a more authentic self-identity. Schor warns that we may need to be prepared for some loss of social status if we curtail taste-based consumption. I don't believe she was suggesting we dump our more extravagant friends but rather that we try to add new ones who might be more accepting of a low-cost lifestyle. Web sites and chat groups on the Internet emphasizing simple living can also provide on-line support.

CHAPTER 3
LEISURE

From each according to his ability, to each according to his needs!
—Louis Blanc
"The organization of work," 1839

THE END GAME IN ECONOMICS

The concept of leisure may seem exotic, since it's so far removed from our everyday world. But it has a history worth exploring. Its modern past begins with the Industrial Revolution, a revolution that simultaneously produced great new wealth and incredible suffering. Dealing with the social impact of this Revolution led to a colossal 200-year struggle between two opposing camps on how to assimilate its impact. The possible uses of leisure played a role in defining those views.

Older generations witnessed the great Cold War between Communism and democratic capitalism,[16] which apparently the latter won. But, democratic capitalism is not without its flaws. As John Maynard Keynes concluded,

---

16   It's important to appreciate that "democratic capitalism" is different from its original free market form or the laissez-faire (let it be) economics of Adam Smith. If free enterprise had not evolved to a more humane form, Western proletariats might have revolted as Marx predicted, and we might all be Communists today.

the major flaw is that *its end is the same as its means*. Materialism, status, self-interest, or whatever it is called, is the primal force that puts the wind in the sails of national economic growth. This is the means of democratic capitalism.

The benefits of this growth are undeniable. Not only has the ownership of wealth since the Industrial Revolution spread from the aristocracy to include a larger bourgeoisie or upper middle class, but history has also shown us time and time again that nations with growing output become more tolerant, more democratic, and more mindful of the disadvantaged. It took decades, after a number of grandiose Five-Year Plans in Communist countries, but eventually capitalism, not Communism, proved to be the more effective path to sustainable growth.

For Communism, the means was a regimented system of central planning with cooperative ownership of production and distribution. Contrary to Marx's expectation, it was not the workers who led the first Communist revolution, but rather a vanguard political organization, called Bolsheviks and headed by Lenin, that had given up hope of waiting for workers to revolt spontaneously. As a result, because of its system of government-favored party members, society was not as egalitarian as Marx might have hoped. The loss of personal freedom during the transition or means period of Communism was the major flaw that Keynes found in this economic system. But he acknowledged in its favor that it did, at least, have a vision of an end game. In *Critique of the Gatha Program* (1875) Karl Marx spelled it out thusly:

> In a higher phase of communist society, after the enslaving subor-
> dination of the individual to the division of labor, and therewith also
> the antithesis between mental and physical labor, has vanished; after
> labor has become not only a means of life but life's prime want; after
> the productive forces have also increased with the all-around develop-
> ment of the individual, and all the springs of co-operative wealth flow

abundantly—only then can the narrow horizon of bourgeois right be crossed in its entirety and society inscribe on its banners:

From each according to his ability, to each according to his needs!

中国人民解放军是毛泽东思想大学校

Marx believed that after a period of reeducation such as Mao's "Cultural Revolution," and a reorganization of government, Communism would lead to a utopian society that would erase class distinctions. Every worker would then be free to mold his or her labor to fit his or her individual talents, rather than the dictates of the owners of capital. Marx saw our greatest meaning in harnessing our unique talents in contributing to the overall economic success of the masses. This would produce greater overall growth for all, as each worker's talents were more effectively utilized, resulting in so much general wealth that material need would be eliminated. Control over one's own labor and the elimination of poverty were parts of the end game. But, also, time ownership would be removed from the factory owner and returned to the worker, although Marx believed that almost everyone would find meaningful work, or self-actualization, as the best use of that time. However "pie in the sky" his vision was, it brought an emotional punch to Communism that many were willing to fight for.

In capitalism, the emphasis is on allowing the invisible hand of self-interest to do its thing, with minimal oversight from government. Capitalists do see a need for government as a kind of referee to keep competition fair, for example, by preventing monopolistic control of the markets and making all competitors subject to the same environmental rules. One problem for Keynes, though, was that *capitalism has no end game*, only more and more consumption. The economist Joseph Stiglitz (*Revisiting Keynes*, p. 54) writes: "There is, in effect, an arms race, a race to consume more and more, working harder and harder, in which no one is the winner."

So where is capitalism headed? Imagine an economist in the midst of the Great Depression (1929–1939) confidently forecasting, as John Maynard Keynes did, that one day the greatest economic problem would be *too much prosperity*. His observations of the unstoppable effects of capital and technology, once they reach critical mass, provided him with the confidence to make this forecast. In *Economic Possibilities for our Grandchildren* (1930), Keynes speculated that at some future date after many years of growth, basic material needs would surely be met for all, and this might spell the end for capitalism. He went on to forecast that by 2030 (100 years later), our Gross Domestic Product (GDP) *per person* after inflation would be four-to-eight times the current output in the progressive nations of his day. Amazingly, we are already well ahead of that forecast.[17] Keynes summarized:

---

17   One economist further extrapolated our current rate of growth out to 2030 and concluded that by then we would achieve output seventeen times the level of 1930! For fifty years the rate of growth of GDP per capita has been 2.9 per percent annually, according to Fabrizio Zilibotti. Extrapolating for the one hundred years to 2030 "corresponds to a 17-fold increase in the standards of living, amounting to more than double Keynes's upper bound." (*Revisiting Keynes*, ed. by Lorenzo Pecchi & Gustavo Piga, 2010, p. 28.)

I draw the conclusion that, assuming no important wars and no important increase in population, the <u>economic</u> <u>problem</u> may be solved, or at least in sight of being solved in a hundred years. . . . Why may you ask is this so startling . . . ? [T]he economic problem, the struggle for subsistence, always has been hitherto the primary, most pressing problem of the human race. . . . If the economic problem is solved, mankind will be deprived of its traditional purpose. What will be the benefit? If one believes at all in the real values of life, the prospect at least opens up the possibility of benefit.

Once we've solved the economic problem, Keynes worried about how we would adjust to the absence of any requirement to work. The only examples he had were the independently wealthy of his day, and he didn't like what he saw. This group had a reputation, mainly, for fox hunting, philandering, and drinking. He speculated that we would first slowly wean ourselves from work by reducing hours and that those who did not follow the existing examples of the wealthy class of his day would benefit the most. The abundance of time could provide the opportunity to find "the real values of life."

Three-hour shifts of a fifteen-hour week may put off the problem for a great while. . . . But it will be those peoples, who can keep alive, and cultivate into a fuller perfection, the art of life itself and do not sell themselves for the means of life, who will be able to enjoy the abundance when it comes.

But as we approach Keynes's theoretical end of the economic problem, cultivating the "art of life" is actually being pushed further away. Time to spend on work and consumption will become more and more valuable monetarily, and consequently, less time will be left to be "wasted" on leisure. As we grow richer, we will find ourselves like the camel unable to pass through the eye of a needle. Modest living is far better suited to leisure pursuits.

> Children, how hard it is for them that trust in riches to enter into the kingdom of God! It is easier for a camel to go through the eye of needle, than for a rich man to enter into the kingdom of God.
> —Mark 10:24–25

I suggest, if we so chose, we could see ourselves as the vanguard of the new capitalism, demonstrating how to live when and if the economic problem is solved, and leisure becomes the norm. In other words, we could lay out an alternative end to just more and more materialism by cultivating, as Keynes put it, "the art of life." For now, however, it seems as though America's appetite for more consumption will never be satiated, even in 2030 at seventeen times (footnote 17) the per capita output of Keynes's day. But, there must be some level so great that a tipping point is reached, perhaps when we have run out of storage space for all our toys, and then we will start looking for alternatives to more and more.

A more ominous possibility is that automation will accelerate to such a degree that the need for human labor will decline faster than new uses for it can be found. In that case, free time, for good or ill, will be forced on us, making cheap but meaningful leisure time critical to our emotional stability. Erik Brynjolfsson and Andrew McAfee argue in *Race Against the Machine* (2011) that increasing obsolescence is precisely what's in store for our workforce.

> General purpose computers [i.e., automation] are directly relevant not only to the 60% of the labor force involved in information-processing tasks but also to more and more of the remaining 40%.

As technology moves into the second half of the chessboard,[18] each successive doubling in power will increase the number of applications where it can affect work and employment. As a result, our skills and institutions will have to work harder and harder to keep up lest more and more of the labor force faces technological unemployment.

David Horsey, September 1, 2013

LEISURE IN PRACTICAL TERMS

Leisure is a part of what is generally considered free time. Leftover free time would not only be after work (including volunteer), but also after personal and property maintenance, including sleep, and after childcare. But, leftover free time includes many activities that would not be considered leisure, such as shopping and consumption of goods, sports, mass and electronic entertainment, socializing with family and friends, and miscellaneous status-motivated

---

18   "Second half of the chess board" is an analogy that can help people understand the power of compounding technology. It is another way to describe "reaching critical mass," when changes that seemed minor in the past suddenly become major. This concept is so important to understand that I feel compelled to refer you directly to the description in *Race Against the Machine*, (p. 18–19) rather than my trying to paraphrase it here.

activities. If you removed the time for these activities, there would be preciously few hours left in the week for the typical hard-working American to engage in "leisure" activities. But if workers managed to fully retire in their sixties and limited their status-related free-time activities, then theoretically, they would have enough time to pursue leisure. In fact, in the past that's what some economists assumed would happen once people could afford it. And, being able to afford leisure seemed within reach for more and more as postwar prosperity unfolded.

Unfortunately, these economists didn't take into account that, for many, more time to just think is a terrifying prospect for those not trained for it. In a study of 146 college students[19], being in a room alone with their thoughts was "so distasteful to two-thirds of men and a quarter of women that they elected to give themselves mild electric shocks rather than sit quietly." In addition, rising productivity in the postwar era not only opened up the possibility of more free time but also the wherewithal for more spending, which was the option most of us chose.

But, how did the concept of leisure originate? The ancient Greeks were the originators of the classic concept of leisure, so we turn to them.

> The Greek word for leisure [*schole*] is the origin of Latin *scola*, German *Schule*, English *school*.
>
> —Joseph Pieper
> *Leisure, the Basis of Culture* (1948, p.3–4.)

> Of possessions, those rather are useful, which bear fruit, those liberal, which tend to enjoyment. By fruitful, I mean which yield income, by enjoyable, where nothing accrues of consequence beyond the using.
>
> —Aristotle

---

19   *Study: Many Are Not Comfortable With Their Thoughts* [University of Virginia]. Michelle Fey Cortez, *Bloomberg News. The Hartford Courant.* July 4, 2014.

For the Greeks leisure was a time for liberal schooling to learn how to enjoy the intrinsic value of the arts, in contrast to useful schooling to learn how to increase income. Liberal schooling could include what we think of today as the liberal arts, but I think in Aristotle's day it mainly meant philosophy or contemplation, plus poetry, music, and perhaps geometry. Geometry, although a science, encompassed *a priori* knowledge, so important in Greek philosophy.

Ancient Athens had a free male citizenship of 25,000 and about 100,000 slaves. This condition allowed for a city-state in which a large portion of the citizens were free from pecuniary concerns and could spend their day in leisure pursuits, if they so chose. Similar circumstances, in which a large portion of the population was free from the need to work for survival, have been rare in history. But some would say, in ancient Athens' case, this produced a leisure class of the wisest citizens who ever lived.

> The classical Greek wanted to be wise. To be wise one had to have leisure. The body needs food and shelter and to get them requires work. But work is neither the noblest nor the most distinguished activity of man. All animals seek food and shelter. Man alone can think, reason, and invent. If some at least could be freed from mundane occupation, they might soar to remarkable heights, and at the same time help lift up to a higher level even those whose workaday life kept them pinned to the ground, where vision is limited.
>
> —Sebastian de Grazia
> *Of Time, Work and Leisure* (1994, p.35)

LEISURE TODAY:

> Leisure has had a bad press. For the puritan it is a source of vice; for the egalitarian a sign of privilege. The Marxist regards leisure as the unjust surplus enjoyed by the few at the expense of the many.

> Nobody in a democracy is at ease with leisure. . . . We mistake leisure with idleness, and work for creativity. . . . Work is the means of life; leisure is the end. Without the end, work is meaningless—a means to a means to a means . . .and so on forever, like Wall Street or Capitol Hill. Leisure is not the cessation of work, but work of a different kind, work restored to its human meaning, as a celebration and as a festival.
>
> —Joseph Pieper
> *Leisure, the Basis of Culture* (1948, p. xi-xii.)

I see leisure as a time to return to liberal studies once you have the financial wherewithal to do so on a sustained basis. It's a time for studies that some may have started in college but were abruptly interrupted by a forty-year career in business. You can find your own way in these studies and will need latitude in modifying the original Greek ideal. For example, we could add history, psychology, language, and comparative religion to Aristotle's list. However, I do not believe that any list that does not include philosophy could be called leisure studies in the traditional sense. "'Liberal arts,' therefore, are ways of human action which have their justification in themselves. . . . Philosophy can be called the most liberal of the liberal arts." (Pieper, p. 22–3.) As noted earlier, Americans are generally not trained in liberal studies, so the prospect of them embracing philosophy is not good, not good at all.

The question becomes: is there any way some could be enticed to climb the learning curve far enough to find liberal studies enjoyable? If so, maybe more would follow. It's important to keep in mind that the leisure approach to learning is nothing like taking Philosophy 101 in college. You can study, unconcerned about your grade or about accumulating facts you're bound to forget. The following anecdote[20] involving Ralph Waldo

---

20   John Albee, *Remembrances of Emerson*, (1901). Thoreau was not a fan of Harvard, even refusing to pay the $5 fee for his diploma. He complained that "Even the poor student studies and is taught political economy [economics], while that economy of living which is synonymous with philosophy is not even seriously professed in our college." (*Walden*)

Emerson and Henry David Thoreau, both Harvard alums, addresses different forms of learning:

> Emerson . . .once remarked to a guest contemplating study at Harvard that the college taught all the branches of knowledge. Quipped Thoreau, "Yes, indeed, all the branches and none of the roots."

The goal of leisure is to understand the roots of knowledge, *to seek out the inspiration behind the liberal arts.* For example, some religions or cults probably have their roots in mystical events that their founders experienced. Then, rituals were built around the founders' interpretation of the meaning of these experiences. Those who come later only see the rituals. I'm interested in the mystical experiences.

The books referenced earlier by Pieper and de Grazia are the only major works on the concept of leisure that I've encountered. What I found missing was any help understanding of how leisure might play out in actual practice. So I can only share my own experience. But my life is only one example, and everyone must find their own path.

I have a set of rituals that I try to follow about three days a week. The rituals take me from waking until early-to-mid afternoon, so three days has been what I can manage. (I imagine that three days a week is similar to what retired golfers can manage for a day of eighteen-hole or "round" of golf.) First thing in the morning, before my objections warm up, I meditate for thirty minutes and then go straight to the YMCA, hop on a treadmill, and attempt to continue meditating while wearing earplugs and keeping my eyes closed. The sustained concentration in meditation on the present moment, more than the walking/running, leaves me with a strong feeling of well-being at the end of the exercise, and in the right state of mind for the rest of the rituals.

Then I study liberal subjects (see Reference section for examples), catch the news on public radio and newspapers, and write, usually at a library. From time to time in my studies, I came across something so moving that I experience a momentary joy akin to transcendence. A prerequisite, at least for me, is moving up a learning curve that enables "light bulb moment" insights across time and across subjects. This is, I think, what John Stuart Mill (mentioned at the beginning of this book) meant by "pleasures of the mind." It's worth pointing out that, aside from YMCA membership fees and some publications not available in the library or online, these rituals are virtually free.

The key to my rituals is belief; they would not work for me otherwise. My belief is the meaning I find in retirement life. It is the product of hours of leisure study and the inspirational transcendent experiences I have uncovered.

Part 1 concludes in Chapter 4 with a couple of stories meant to illustrate how a search for signs of transcendence can help guide your leisure studies. Part 2 offers a much deeper look; please stay with me.

CHAPTER FOUR

TRANSCENDENCE

The following scene takes place in virgin wilderness near the Great Lakes around 1759. Four travelers are awestruck when they happen upon a break in the oppressive forest that has surrounded them for days.

The sublimity connected with vastness is familiar to every eye . . .as he gazes into the depths of the illimitable void . . . . With feelings akin to this admiration and awe—the offspring of sublimity—were the different characters with which the action of this tale must open, gazing on the scene before them. . . . Towards the west, in which the faces of the party were turned, and in which alone much could be seen, the eye ranged over an ocean of leaves. . . . It was the vastness of the view, the nearly unbroken surface of verdure that contained the principle of grandeur.

—James Fenimore Cooper
The Pathfinder, 1840, p. 1–3

When I first read these lines from the opening paragraphs of *The Pathfinder*, it struck a chord deep within, and I experienced a strong feeling of *déjà vu*. But when? I had never seen wilderness. Finally, my memory search took me way back to around kindergarten age. I was exploring the partially developed neighborhood around my family's new home when I came to the "frontier" at a wheat field. The wheat was eye level and blocked my view of the beyond. But, when I climbed up a small knoll at the edge of the field, several acres of wheat, my "ocean of leaves," opened before me and seemed to stretch to the horizon. To one of my small size, the field seemed "illimitable." I determined to embark on a voyage into the unexplored depths of that field, leaving everything in my old life behind. I was free. What unimaginable wonders awaited me?

The memory of that delicious feeling of awe and wonder had lain dormant until my reading of *The Pathfinder*. That event, though, initiated and confirmed my belief in the possibility of transcendence,[21] that is, that there may be a better reality that transcends our workaday world.

My father had similar beliefs, I imagine, although he wouldn't have used the term "transcendence." He told me stories of growing up on a farm in North Carolina and his fascination reading about the exploration of Africa. He especially loved stories about Henry Morton Stanley, whose explorations of the Dark Continent around 1880 into unknown areas of the Congo had taken place only thirty years earlier. But, my father grew up, had a family to raise, and responsibilities to meet. Then one day in his sixties, with his children self-supporting and his business well-established, he decided to return to his childhood dreams. At first, it was travel to typical, and then to more exotic, parts of the world. It was as if he had to circle around his real dream,

---

21   "This experience typically evokes a perception that human reality extends beyond the physical body and its psychosocial boundaries. A principal characteristic of this experience involves transcendence of one's personal identity and dissolution of a primary conscious focus on grounding in one's ego."
"The Transcendent Experience," Jeff Levine and Lea Steele, *Explore*, 2005.

because he still wasn't sure it was OK. Later, on a trip to Africa, he arranged for a short hunting safari into wilderness areas of Tanzania. Meanwhile, I had sat through many boring hours of watching slides of his previous trips, but I will never forget the photograph of his first kill on that African safari. With rifle in hand, he was squatting, an older Hemmingway look-alike, next to a dead antelope. I saw in that moment an expression of uncommon joy on his face that I had never seen in the twenty-five years I had known him. My sense that something profound had happened to cause that expression was palpable. I like to believe that coming this close to his childhood dreams was a transcendent experience for him. He certainly returned to the scene often enough, taking several more safaris over the years and stuffing his attic and garage with animal heads.

My father had taken a physical journey to a spiritual experience. His African path would not work for me, even if I could afford it.

It is instructive, though, that he took care of family, career, and status-in-the-community issues first before experimenting with his childhood wonder lust. I have always suspected intuitively that searching for transcendence would probably never be successful as a part-time sideshow. The instinctive drive for materialistic status is just too demanding of one's time and energy. Usually, only when a degree of financial independence has been achieved, can one afford to give this search primary attention.[22]

I believe there are intellectual paths that can lead you partway to transcendence. Philosophy, as a pathway to the sublime, was first developed by the Greeks 2,500 years ago. Other alternative or complementary intellectual paths often suggested include contemplation, religion and theology, meditation,

---

22 It is not that many haven't sought to lead a more meaningful life while ignoring materialistic status. A career in the clergy is an obvious example. Others have given up Wall Street careers to work on farms in Vermont, joined communes or Bohemian communities, or simply become committed to a "voluntary simplicity" movement. My experience with a few financial clients who tried this is that (clergy aside) there is a high degree of recidivism. Most people need their status.

and aesthetics, especially music. My approach is to start with the philosophy of the ancient Greeks and then to follow this thread to the recent past with reference to other paths from time to time.

Ancient Greek philosophy tried to encompass a wide range of knowledge, including mathematics, science, ethics, and government. Because of my overriding interest in transcendence, the coverage of the philosophy thread will concentrate on the non-empirical and the metaphysical.[23] By sifting through the myriad paths and the contradictions in philosophy over the years, I hope to assemble a coherent set of ideas that works for me. This won't be easy. I know most people have determined that the current materialistic and non-spiritual view of life works fine. So, I feel like the soldier in a marching platoon who tries to convince himself he's the only one in step.

Why don't most people buy into philosophy? To begin with, some skeptics believe that there has been no significant progress in metaphysics since Plato's Academy in ancient Greece. And even that knowledge is suspect. Herbert Spencer (1820–1903) believed that the reason Plato's masterpiece, *The Republic*, received so much acclaim was because the public didn't really understand it and didn't want to appear ignorant. Mr. Spencer assured his public that he understood it and that there was nothing to it.

Also, it's hard to use philosophy as a personal guide when the philosophers themselves can't agree. There seems to be little captured territory, such as we have in science. As soon as one philosopher is recognized for uncovering new insights, another one later tries to debunk those new insights. An exception that others have for the most part left alone is Immanuel Kant, whom we will meet later. Unfortunately, he almost closed the door forever on metaphysics.

---

23   The term "metaphysical" causes confusion for many. Its origin was in reference to the writings of Aristotle that came after (meta in Greek) his writings on matter and natural science (physics). Greek philosophers tried to explain as much as possible by natural, materialistic, causes and then assign the rest to metaphysics. What has real existence? Do thoughts have real existence? Is there any method besides observation to answer these questions? Is there a part of reality that transcends our normal powers of awareness? These are metaphysical questions.

Finally, if philosophy provided superior insights into the true nature of the world and mankind, why were so many famous philosophers so flawed and unhappy? However, the average person will simply claim to see no value in philosophy because it has no monetary or status value.

To bother with philosophy, as an amateur, you'd need to truly believe, and not just give lip service to, the idea that certain types of knowledge or experience can have a spiritual value that may be more meaningful and permanent than material values. If you come to this with that kind of belief, then perhaps philosophy has something to offer. Because uncertainties and contradictions are part of the territory, we may need to put our own spin on what philosophers have said to make it work for us. With religion, the details are provided. One can just accept the total package as is.

Philosophy is more of a do-it-yourself project.[24] And it helps to begin at the beginning with as few assumptions as possible.[25]

---

24   Ralph Waldo Emerson wrote: "Make your own Bible. Select and collect all the words and sentences that in all your reading have been to you like the blast of triumph out of Shakespeare, Seneca, Moses, John and Paul."

25   Sir Francis Bacon wrote: "Another error is an impatience of doubt, and the haste to assertion without due and mature suspension of judgment..,. [S]o it is with contemplation; *if a man shall begin with certainties, he shall end with in doubts; but if he will be content to begin in doubts he shall end in certainties.*" [Emphasis mine.] *Of the Proficience and Advancement of Learning* (1605)

THE SEARCH FOR MEANING

CHAPTER FIVE

THE DAWN OF PHILOSOPHY

Human beings have certain advantages over other animals that brought them to the top of the food chain and provided them with relative security. Some of these are:

- A superior ability to learn and to adapt to changing environments
- Highly developed abstract reasoning that permits them to form general concepts about their situation
- Superior communication, language, to enable sharing information for the benefit of all

More intelligent animals, like chimpanzees, have less developed, stunted, versions of these abilities. One advantage for humans that may be unique is sentience, the awareness of one's individuality apart from the environment. Nevertheless, for all their superior knowledge, there is still much people do not know. With imperfect knowledge, we've had to make decisions, which in early history, often had life-or-death consequences. Everyone's security was improved as people banded together in larger and larger tribes. This not only provided mutual defense but also sharing of knowledge.

As tribal knowledge accumulated, and before writing was invented, a concern arose about how to preserve important lessons learned in a way that could be handed down to younger generations. Some mechanical skills could be passed on through training in a master-apprentice relationship. But even primitives also had to deal with ontological questions. For example, they observed that people obviously undergo profound changes when they die. Was the missing element their spirit? What happens to that spirit when it leaves the body? Why, despite one's best efforts, do crops sometimes fail? Has an unseen entity been offended? In general, why do bad things happen to good people? There were life-and-death consequences to questions like these, and "don't know" was not an acceptable answer. There was a great desire to produce knowledge about things beyond their power to know.

Someone had to be able to bring order to the chaos. The shaman[26] evolved to fill this role. He was often the oldest member of a tribe, which made a kind of sense. It was believed that if he'd survived so long, he must know something others didn't. From time to time, tribes did gain insight into ontological issues that they wanted to pass on to future generations. One method was storytelling and sagas, passed down verbally by repetition. Some, like the stories of King Arthur, Beowulf, and the Trojan War, survived long enough to be written down. Dance, song, and mythology were also used to preserve a people's heritage before writing. The earliest religions, like Hinduism, were preserved by requiring members of the Brahmin class, starting as early as age five, to memorize the entire *Vedas* by heart through a process of chanting recitations.

---

26 We still have shamans today. They are called "gurus" like people who claim to know the short-term future direction of the stock market. Investors will pay serious money to listen to them, because not knowing is unthinkable.

About 2,000 to 3,000 years ago, several major religions were founded or revealed[27] and helped people achieve some peace with the unknown. An important feature of western mythology and religion was the personification of some of the unknown as gods. They were recognizably human-like. The gods were usually male, sometimes with human vices (like the Olympian and Norse gods) but usually with superhuman virtues. In Christianity there are frequent references to kings, kingdoms, lords, and fealty.[28]

Outside of religion, though, a different method of addressing ontological issues, called philosophy, was developed in Greece in the middle of the last millennium BCE.

ANCIENT PHILOSOPHY

Against the backdrop of mythology and early religion, the Hellenic society, beginning around 600 BCE, developed a unique approach to answering life's essential questions. It was called philosophy, meaning love of knowledge. Everywhere else in the known world, people went to priests or shamans for

---

27   Paul Tillich in *Theology of Culture* (1959) writes that religion does not originate within man "as a creative element of the human spirit." If that were true, the monotheistic religions that came to man only a couple of thousand years ago would not be eternal. Rather, theologians believe God is the active agent, providing religion "as a gift of divine revelation." He reveals it to a few select individuals, who then spread their understanding of the divine message by ministering to the faithful and by the written word.

28   Some would argue (and I don't disagree) that Western religions' representation of God with human characteristics is metaphorical. It is meant to help believers understand some basic truths about their religion. The truths are more important than the methods used to teach them. "I believe so that I may understand" (Anselm of Canterbury). Despite our vast reasoning power, God is beyond human powers of comprehension. A crude analogy is the relationship of a dog to its owner. To the dog, the master must seem like a god. This human master can do things the poor dog can't remotely comprehend. Food magically appears. They're whisked to faraway locations in a moving box in minutes. They're protected from the elements in a magnificent tree-high structure. How does Fido deal with such an omnipotent being? The only way he knows how. He treats him like the leader of the pack, an instinct passed down from his wolf pack ancestors. When the master appears, he grows excited, wags his tail violently, and rolls over on his back, legs in the air, as a sign of submission. This is based on knowledge of rituals appropriate for the leader of the pack, and by inference, an omnipotent being.

answers to their questions about life and living. But the Greeks had an odd view of their gods. They believed that their gods didn't much care what humans did as long as temples were built and sacrifices were made. The gods were much more interested in their own intrigues and had little concern for man. They were capricious and unpredictable and even mated with mortals. For their part, the Greeks worshiped the gods, offered sacrifices, and tried in general to keep on their good side. But they didn't look to them, or their priests, for advice on daily living. Philosophers, without input from priests, began to tackle some of the metaphysical issues formerly addressed on an ad hoc basis by mythology, sagas, and drama. However, philosophers addressed these issues in a much more systematic fashion, trying to encompass the entire subject matter. Also, Greeks, particularly Athenians, were a naturally skeptical lot because of their exposure to a wide diversity of cultures encountered in their seafaring economy. Assertions of dogmatic opinion were taken with a shrug; they had heard it all before. This broad exposure made some Greeks question whether anything was absolutely true and not subject to conditions of some sort. An early school of thinkers called "Cynics" developed. They were the doubting Thomases of their day, who wouldn't believe anything unless it could be irrefutably demonstrated. They refused to accept edits from a priest or some other so-called authority at face value.[29]

Greek philosophers wanted to find enduring truths, to go beyond the Cynics and Sophists who believed all knowledge was relative and situational.

---

29   Another skeptical group, besides the Cynics, and another roadblock for philosophers searching for ultimate truth, were the "Sophists." They were basically agnostic when it came to Truth, because to them it was all relative. "Man is the measure of all things," i.e., whatever worked to the advantage of man was truth. Sophists had evolved to meet a need. In a democracy like Athens, decisions were often made by an assembly of citizens numbering in the hundreds—with rotating membership. Oratory and debating skills were in great demand. Sophists were basically professional trainers in rhetoric. They taught their clients how to make attractive arguments that were likely to impress large audiences. "Truth" was not the object, but rather what could be sold as truth to large audiences. A number of Sophists achieved great fame and were "rock stars" of their day. Some of the most famous of these were foils in many of the dialogues attributed to Socrates by Plato.

In this skeptical environment they tried to be rigorous in their attempts to justify what they saw as truths. They understood how easy it was to be beguiled into a pleasing-sounding philosophy that turned out later to be only wishful thinking. They relied on logic and dialectical discourse to test their ideas in a public forum. Later, with Aristotle, empirical analysis would be employed for lasting knowledge of the natural world.

Finally, the findings of these philosophers would be written down and documented so that others could gain from, and perhaps add to, the growing body of knowledge. They laid the foundation of enduring knowledge about the nature of our world. Now let's take a brief look at three of the best known of these Greek philosophers.

PLATO (427–347 BCE)

Plato believed that philosophers should be kings. But why? Philosophers are intellectuals, usually with little practical experience compared to, say, a seasoned manager from the military or the bureaucracy. Philosophers, though, supposedly have access to true knowledge, knowledge that doesn't change with fads or public opinion. The public is better led when their leaders have special knowledge of what's truly in everyone's best interest and who are not influenced by money, fame, or other self-serving motivations.

What exactly was this special knowledge that Plato felt was available only to a few gifted individuals, known as "men of gold," who were to master this knowledge after decades of intensive training? To illustrate this special knowledge of philosophers, Plato used an allegory called "The Cave." In this story the general populace lived in a cave and were, by nature, sensualists,[30] believing only what they could see. They were shackled in place and in a

---

30 Sensualist: One who believes everything he sees and only what he sees. He is ripe for manipulation from outsiders using misleading images (like TV ads) and can also be the victim of his or her own self-delusional tendencies. Our senses alone, though, can never apprehend ultimate truths.

position where their only view was one wall of the cave. On this wall their captors, behind and above them, used a light source to project, for purposes of manipulation, shadows of various objects. Not surprisingly, these shackled men with no other experience of life assumed these shadows were real and were the only reality. One, though, broke loose from his shackles and, by a laborious and terrifying journey through unlit tunnels, found his way above-ground to the sunlight. He was momentarily blinded[31] because his eyes were accustomed to operating in dim light. But, as his eyes adjusted, he began to see sharper definition, color, and the real objects of the world. He was transformed and infused with true knowledge. There could be no doubt that this was true reality, not the shadows on the wall. He rushed back to bring his revelations to his comrades below. They listened to what he had to say and determined that he was quite mad. Everyone knew for a fact that the shadows on the wall never appeared in the way he described. Moral: philosophers make better leaders because they know the forces truly at work in the world and, therefore, can make better judgments in the best interests of everyone. These judgments will be in harmony with the true reality that only they can see. But don't bother trying to explaining that reality to the public. They don't have the wherewithal to grasp it.

We begin with Plato's cave as an allegory. One can't come to the light while holding on to the shackles of old knowledge, shadows on the wall. We first have to deny comfortable group think and then make a long, difficult climb to find new knowledge. When we do acquire this new knowledge, there will be no doubt, because of the temporarily blinding nature of the experience. This describes a kind of permanent enlightenment. Perhaps it's a useful metaphor for the superior knowledge of philosopher-kings, but it's short on details about

---

31   "The light which puts out our eyes is darkness to us. Only that day dawns to which we are awake. There is more day to dawn. The sun is but a morning star." Henry David Thoreau, *Walden* (1854), final words.

the paths or tunnels to this knowledge other than putting in decades of study. It is, though, an early description of a transcendent experience.

After a lecture on Plato's cave, John Immerwahr, a professor of philosophy at Villanova University, was asked how we could be sure we had philosophically escaped the cave and reached enlightenment. Dr. Immerwahr replied that if the questioner had to ask the question, he was probably still in the cave. To illustrate, he told a story about overnight mountain climbing. When his climbing party broke camp, it was still pre-dawn, and there was a heavy mist. They climbed for an hour or so in the dark. At a plateau, some wondered if they had reached the peak. But no, even in the poor light, they could see another rise ahead. After climbing up an outcropping, they were sure they had reached the top. But with more light and thinning mist, they could see more mountain ahead. Climbing further, they suddenly burst through the cloud cover. The sun was just clearing the horizon. The peak was there against a blue sky. With the sun at that angle, the shadow from the peak stretched out for fifty to sixty miles on the tops of the clouds. When you leave Plato's cave and reach the sunlight, you will know.

Besides the metaphysical belief that true reality lies beyond our everyday senses, the philosophers of Plato's Academy also assumed the existence of a soul, a belief inherited from the past. The soul possessed ultimate truths and resided in a particular body for only a time. When we try to grasp these truths through our senses, we distort them. For example, the Pythagorean Theorem, $A^2 + B^2 = C^2$, never changes, but our conscious attempts to represent this truth by drawing a triangle is imperfect and subject to distortion. The souls in rational beings possess truths that never could be discovered experimentally. "Everyone has experience, but few are wise."

The "dialectical" approach of Socrates and Plato, as opposed to the experimental approach to knowledge, is by open discussion. The goal is not new knowledge as much as *recalled* knowledge of the soul. In the great schism between science and philosophy, the scientist, who adheres to the experimental approach, has to concede one point. There are unchanging truths, at least in mathematics and geometry, that are known without resort to experiment. For example, some intuitive discoveries in mathematics have been confirmed empirically much later, sometimes centuries later, after the development of improved methods of observation. This notion of inherited knowledge of the soul was also addressed by Socrates and Aristotle.

SOCRATES (469–399 BCE)

Socrates demonstrated this type of ultimate *a priori* knowledge, some two thousand years before Descartes, in a famous dialogue, described by Plato. The celebrated Sophist, Meno, was visiting Athens. In this dialogue he tried to convince Socrates that his search for enduring knowledge of the soul was meaningless; it either didn't exist or no one would know where to look. Accompanying Meno at the time was a slave boy, who, Meno confirmed had had no formal schooling. By drawing triangles in the sand, while asking the boy questions, Socrates was able to demonstrate to Meno that the boy understood, on an intuitive level, the principles of the Pythagorean Theorem. Socrates believed that some of our knowledge is reminiscence; it resides in our souls. This knowledge is not subject to variation, based on history or culture, unlike our knowledge of material reality. This reminiscence of eternal truths may be accessible through introspection and dialogue.

ARISTOTLE (384–322 BCE)

Aristotle's metaphysics grew out of his more practical interest in biology. Everything in nature is moved by an inner urge to become something greater than it is. To really know what something is, one needed to know more than only its observable features. A statue can serve as an example. The material in the statue may be marble. Overall, it may appear similar to a man; and one can observe the act of the sculptor chiseling out the details. But, we still don't know the statue. Its most important feature is still unknown: its cause, which is unobservable. That cause is the idea of the ultimate statue in the mind of the sculptor. Aristotle's implication is that we exist not because of what we see around us but because of the working of the mind of an unseen creator.

CHAPTER SIX

REDISCOVERING PHILOSOPHY

THE GREAT SCHISM

Aristotle spent an estimated twenty years at Plato's Academy and was well versed in Plato's metaphysics. But he was more comfortable with materialistic and naturalistic knowledge. His classic writing on natural science was titled *Physics*. In the early Middle Ages, there was a revival of interest in academic study of the ancient Greeks, mainly within the Roman Catholic Church. One of the Church's goals was to try to reconcile classical philosophy with Christian theology. These Catholic academics, called scholastics, came to refer to Aristotle's later writings as his metaphysics, simply meaning that they came after his *Physics*. Subsequently, the whole portion of philosophy concerned with the nonmaterial came to be known as metaphysics. This part of classical philosophy undoubtedly gave the scholastics grave problems of reconciliation with Church dogma. It deals with essentially spiritual questions about humanity. First are the ontological questions such as:

- What has real existence?
- What kind of entity am I?
- Do Plato's forms have real existence?

Second are the epistemological questions:

- What do we know?
- How do we know it?
- Is there any method, other than observation, to answer these questions?
- In other words, does *a priori* knowledge exist?

To the last two questions, Protagoras, Socrates, and Plato, among classical philosophers, would answer, "Yes." Democritus (460–370 BCE) was among the first to answer, "No." To him everything was ultimately reducible to molecular atoms and the void. In fact, the list of philosophers on the "no" side was quite extensive. The Cynics and Sophists would also vote "no," along with modern philosophers, a few of whom we will meet later, starting with Sir Francis Bacon. In my opinion, there are also agnostics on this question, too. I would put Aristotle in that camp. The existentialists of our own era feel that metaphysics, right or wrong, is simply irrelevant, compared to the overarching importance of basic individual human existence.

Raphael's famous "School of Athens" painting in the Vatican includes many of the classical Greek philosophers. The two central figures are Plato and Aristotle. Plato is pointing up, signifying the importance of universals and metaphysics. Aristotle is pointing down, signifying the importance of empirical knowledge. During their lives, philosophy included both types of knowledge. But, when interest returned to secular knowledge before and during the Renaissance, philosophy and science became forever divided.

Philosophy crested with the lives of Socrates, Plato, and Aristotle and declined in influence in the pre-Christian ancient world, save for some brief interest in the Stoic philosophy of Zeno and the Epicurean philosophy of Epicurus.

Religion and philosophy usually don't mix easily. When Christianity became the official religion of Rome in 380 CE, philosophy ceased to receive serious consideration as a guide in people's lives. The vibrancy of the true

Christian believer swept the ancient philosophies off the stage. After the fall of Rome, personal security and the opportunities for safe commerce that came from a strong central government were lacking. That environment left little opportunity for leisure time to pursue philosophy. The Christian monasteries did aid philosophy, though, by preserving some of the ancient texts. A few Christian thinkers, like St. Augustine and St. Francis, recognized the importance of Greek philosophical writings and tried to incorporate some of the ideas into their theology. Logic was their special favorite. The ultimate expression of the use of Greek logic to try to prove the tenets of Christian theology was *The Summa Theologica* by St. Thomas Aquinas, which had reached more than 3,000 pages and was still unfinished at his death in 1274.[32]

BACON (1561–1626)

When life began to return to philosophy outside the Roman Catholic Church, it was in pursuit of practical and materialistic knowledge. Sir Francis Bacon found in *Organon*, Aristotle's treatise on logic, what he been looking for to bring order to the many techniques of scientific inquiry that existed in his day. He laid out the modern version of Aristotle's techniques in the *Novum Organum,* "new instrument." His motto was that if you want to know something, go out and look at it. Forget theology and theorizing about it like the Church was likely to do. Bacon also had little use for metaphysics.

> Man, as the minister and interpreter of nature, does and understands as much as the observations on the order of nature . . . permit him; and neither knows nor is capable of more.

---

32 The term "logic chopping" is sometimes used to describe this kind of argument. I found—after six hours of listening to compact disks that used logic to "prove" God's existence and the afterlife—that this type of persuasion becomes extremely tedious. It seems unlikely that more than a handful of people have ever been rationally convinced to become Christians by this method.

This observation was a good depiction of the fork in the road that forever severed science from philosophy and metaphysics. In the years that followed, Hobbes, Newton, Galileo, Malthus, Hume, and Darwin all took the science fork. They took it with the confidence that, because of the undeniable advances they were making, human life in the future would be improved through rational science. A modern example of this confidence is DuPont's old slogan, "Better living through chemistry." Anything lost by ignoring metaphysics would hardly be noticed.

With the emergence of non-philosophical scientific inquiry, spearheaded by Bacon, there was a new force outside the Church to bring Western Europe into the early years of the modern era. The Roman Catholic Church and its universities had held the monopoly on knowledge, unchallenged for the thousand or so years of the Middle Ages. But, the scientific approach was producing impressive and undeniable advances in practical knowledge. The Church, though, still held people's hearts, if not their heads. So, scientists had to be careful in trying to expand scientific knowledge without conflicting with Church canon. The trial for heresy and the subsequent recantation (1633) of Galileo is one example of this conflict. Galileo used observations from his improved telescope to support Copernicus's theory of a helio-centric universe. He was forced to publically "abjure, curse, and detest" his "mistaken" belief that the earth revolved around the sun. His writings were banned, and he remained under house arrest until his death in 1642.

LIFE SLOWLY RETURNS TO METAPHYSICS

Church scholars of the Middle Ages studied the Greek classics to learn logic and dialectic techniques in hopes of building a logical argument for Christianity. They must have encountered Greek metaphysics in their research. But, trying to advance metaphysics was much more difficult without running directly counter to Church dogma. Scientists could at least produce physical proof of their advancements. It was harder to prove theories about ontology and epistemology.

DESCARTES (1596–1650)

René Descartes, a younger contemporary of Bacon, is acknowledged as perhaps being the first to significantly address a question of ontology since the Greeks, a gap of 2,000 years. Few, if any, of the followers of Bacon or Newton took metaphysics seriously during this period. One needed credentials in the fields of mathematics, geometry, or science to receive any attention by the intelligentsia. Descartes, as it happened, was an accomplished mathematician, so he clearly understood his contemporaries' hydraulic or materialistic explanation of phenomena, but he felt abstract thought was something different. He believed that here, at least, there was knowledge not acquired through the scientific methods of empirical observation and experimentation.

But, how could he make a convincing argument that even the materialists would have to accept? They would argue that any knowledge one thinks is gained outside of scientific inquiry is open to self-serving manipulation or deceit—from others or oneself. Therefore, that kind of knowledge couldn't be trusted. Descartes' famous argument was that there was at least one thing one knows *a priori* independent of experience, and without any possibility of deceit. *You know you must exist as a rational being.* Why? Because how could a non-rational non-being be deceived? (Socrates used a different approach to establish the existence of *a priori* knowledge. See "Socrates" above.)

"I think, therefore I am." This is probably the most misinterpreted quote in philosophy. It doesn't mean that thinking is the essence of one's being, as in the following joke: "Descartes goes into a bar and orders an apéritif. When he finishes, the bartender asks him if he'd like another. Descartes replies, 'I think not' and disappears."

SPINOZA (1632–1677)

Baruch Spinoza was eighteen when Descartes died. He was heavily influenced by Descartes' writings and was also well-trained in mathematics. In fact, he believed that philosophy couldn't match up with science unless it used the forms of mathematics and geometry to express itself.[33] An important pantheistic influence on Spinoza was Giordano Bruno (1548–1600), who provided a good example of the risks of being a metaphysical philosopher during this period. Bruno was burned at the stake in 1600 by the Roman Catholic Inquisition[34] after a judgment of heresy for claiming that God and all creatures were one.

Spinoza, as philosopher, was excommunicated for heresy at the age of twenty-four—not by the Catholic Church—but by the Jewish Ecclesiastical Council. His Jewish community was very concerned about the opinions Spinoza expressed about God for fear that they might offend their Christian hosts in Amsterdam. This city was one of the few relative safe havens for Jews in Europe during the Spanish Inquisition (1478–1834). Many had recently arrived from Spain, where they'd been presented with a harsh ultimatum: either convert to Christianity or be expelled, with all their possessions expropriated. Fortunately, the Christians in Amsterdam were tolerant enough to allow expelled Jews to settle there. Christian and Jewish orthodoxy effectively shut down independent expression of opinion in spiritual matters except for a few brave or foolhardy philosophers like Bruno and Spinoza. Jewish excommunication was an extremely serious matter for Spinoza. It was not only being barred from attending services in the synagogue. No one in his Jewish community, including his family, was allowed to interact with him in any way.

---

33   On the gates of his Academy, Plato inscribed the following words: "Let no man ignorant of geometry enter here."

34   The Inquisition took the opportunity of Bruno's execution to portray a particularly sick form of either compassion or humor. It proclaimed that they chose burning at the stake as the more "merciful" punishment, for this method could be carried out "without the shedding of any blood."

Hereby then are all admonished that none may hold conversation with him by word of mouth, nor hold communication with him by writing; that no one do him any service, no one abide under the same roof with him, no one approach within four cubits length of him, and no one read any document dictated or written by his hand.

One zealous member of the synagogue decided to ignore the edict about approaching "within four cubits length of him" and attempted to gain favor by stabbing him to death. Obviously, living in his old community was no longer an option, so Spinoza fled to the outskirts to board with the family from a splinter sect of Christians, the Mennonites. Thereafter, he squeezed out a subsistence living, grinding eyeglass lens in his second-floor flat.

Spinoza's joy was his devoted study of and writing about philosophy.[35] Unfortunately, it was too dangerous to try to publish anything he wrote. He finished the first of his four major works in 1665, nine years after his excommunication. He didn't try to publish it for another ten years, shortly before his death. Other authors attempting to publish similar material had been sent to jail, in one case for ten years. Most of Spinoza's work was published

---

35   There have been many unheralded amateur philosophers through the centuries, including those following Bohemian traditions in Paris and elsewhere in the nineteenth century. In our day, we have Eric Hoffer and Colin Wilson among those that come to mind in my limited knowledge of iconoclasts. Eric Hoffer was blind for several years after a fall down a flight of stairs. When his eyesight miraculously returned at age fifteen, he became a voracious reader, determined to read everything he could in case he ever lost his sight again. Poor and with limited formal education, he worked odd jobs, with his last job as a longshoreman in Los Angeles for twenty-five years before retiring at age sixty-five. Most of his spare time was spent in libraries educating himself. He became an accomplished and original philosopher, and published the *True Believer* in 1951. This book is considered a classic on the origin and psychological nature of mass movements, both religious and non-religious. Colin Wilson, whom I will have more to say about later, worked in a tax office in Leicester, England, which did not afford him the leisure he needed to study and write. So, he quit and thereafter took odd jobs like washing dishes at night before retiring to his waterproof sleeping bag on the Hampstead Heath. He did his study and writing during the day in public places like the British Museum. His classic, *The Outsider*, was published in 1956.

posthumously. But, his reputation while still alive did spread by other means, and many came to converse with him in his humble flat.

Late in life he acquired some fame as a thinker and was even offered the chair of philosophy at the University of Heidelberg. The offer came from the royal ruler of the principality along with the prince's personal opinion "that the position offered the most perfect freedom of philosophizing, which His Highness feels assured you would not abuse by calling into question the established religion of the state." Spinoza replied:

> The offer, too, is much enhanced in value in my eyes by the freedom of philosophizing attached to it. . . . But I do not know within the precise limits that same freedom of philosophizing would have to be restrained, so that I do not seem to interfere with the established religion of the principality . . . . You see, therefore, honored sir, that I do not look for any higher worldly position than that which I do now enjoy; and that for the love of the quiet which I think I cannot otherwise secure, I must abstain from entering upon a career of a public teacher.

Spinoza sacrificed all for his "freedom of philosophizing," but in the end, he felt he got the better deal.

> I could see the many advantages acquired from honor and riches, and that I should be disbarred from acquiring those things if I wished seriously to investigate a new matter. . . . But, the more one possesses of either of them [honor and riches], the more the pleasure is increased, and the more one is in consequence encouraged to increase them; whereas if at any time our hope is frustrated, there arises in us deep pain. . . . But the love towards a thing eternal and infinite alone feeds the mind with a pleasure secure from all pain. . . . The greatest good is the knowledge of the union the mind has with the whole of the universe.

What was Spinoza's metaphysics? He believed that our world consists of two conditions: mode and substance. Mode is the individual thing or phenomenon. But underneath individual appearance is substance. Substance doesn't mean material substance, but the unobservable nature of the thing that eternally and unchangeably is—in other words, its essence. Mode is a transitory representation of the underlying substance. For example, a circle drawn on paper is an object that can be erased, but the concept of a circle and the mathematical constant of pi is forever. Spinoza, though, differs from Plato in identifying substance with nature and God, not some otherworldly realm of forms. Nature and God are the active and permanent agents of substance beneath the passive and transitory appearances of mode.

> Like substance, God is the causal agent or process, the underlying condition of all things, the law and structure of the world. This concrete [visual] universe of modes and things is to God as a bridge is to its design, its structure, and the laws of mathematics and mechanics to which it is built; these are the sustaining basis, the underlying condition, the substance of the bridge; without them it would fall. And like the bridge, the world itself is sustained by its structure and its laws; it is upheld in the hand of God.

Spinoza held that God was the ultimate cause and substance of the world. One cannot help wonder why this philosophy was considered so dangerous to the Catholic (and Jewish) church that his writings couldn't be published. Perhaps this God was too amorphous and lacked the characteristics of God promulgated by the established religions. A God that did not include human characteristics[36] was unacceptable. To a correspondent who wrote to him objecting to his impersonal interpretation of the nature of God, Spinoza replied:

---

36 "On the last day of creation, God said, 'Let us make man in our image, in our likeness'." (Genesis 1:26). Today, I believe theologians interpret this to mean that God made man in his spiritual image—not his material image—by giving him a soul.

When you say that I allow not in God the operations of see-
ing, hearing, observing and the like . . . you know not what sort of
God mine is, I thence conjecture that you believe there is no greater
perfection than such as can be explained by the attributes aforesaid.
I do not marvel at it; for I believe that a triangle, if it could speak,
would in like manner say God is eminently triangular, and a circle
that divine nature is eminently circular; and thus would every one,
describe his own attributes to God.

Even though an image of God by Michelangelo is painted on the Sistine
Chapel ceiling in the Vatican, does anyone really know the appearance of
God? What can we know? But, because of the human need to fill in gaps
of religious knowledge, there will always be "experts" willing to provide
answers. And, people will accept those particular answers that resonate
within them.

Spinoza also gave a lot of thought to the concept of "free will."[37] Most
people, he thought, possessed very little of it, and in this belief, I believe that
he anticipated Schopenhauer in a way to be discussed later.

There is in the mind no absolute or free will; but the mind is
determined in willing this or that by a cause, and this by another,
and so on to infinity. . . . Men think themselves free because they are

---

37　Philosophers believe in either a strong or weak form of free will. Spinoza and
Schopenhauer believed in a weak form: Man's will is determined by the innate needs of
the species to survive, procreate, and hoard (for security), and to seek pleasure and avoid
pain. What's left is but a meek reasoning faculty. In the weak form of free will, the reasoning faculty is employed like an obedient clerk to produce rationalizations for the largely
predetermined course of action and to manage the details of execution. The clerk may
think he is acting independently until he chooses a course of action that runs counter to
the will. For example, he might reason things out carefully, using well-tuned methods of
analysis, and determine that he needs to change certain of his personal habits. This familiar
process is how New Year's resolutions—like losing weight—are born. Then, he wonders
a month or two later what happened to his logical resolutions as the old habits return.

conscious of their volitions and desires. But they are ignorant of the causes by which they are led to wish and desire.

Spinoza felt that he had found his own salvation and held out hope for others.

> For an ignorant man [sensualist], besides being agitated in many ways by external causes never enjoys one true satisfaction of the mind. . . . On the contrary the wise man, in so far as he is considered such, is scarcely moved in spirit [by external causes]; he is conscious of himself, of God, and things by a certain external necessity; he never ceases to be, and always enjoys satisfaction of mind. If the road I have shown to lead to this is very difficult, it can yet be discovered.

Spinoza had very admirable characteristics: unassuming, utterly courageous, and very much at peace with his world. To try to follow his road to transcendence, you would probably want to begin by reading his *Ethics,* published posthumously in 1677. While only about 200 pages long, the book is reportedly very dense and needs to be read slowly with copious help from commentaries, and then carefully reread. But the philosophy historian Will Durant promises: "When you have finished reading it a second time you will remain forever a lover of philosophy."

VOLTAIRE (1694–1778)

François-Marie Arouet, who wrote under the pen name of Voltaire, was a philosopher who appeared on the world stage as the Church was just starting to lose its stranglehold on European thought. In his early years Voltaire had little public disagreement with the Church. To gain admittance to the French Academy, he trumpeted his Catholicism and said and did what was expected to gain widespread acceptance in French society. But he had also read Rousseau[38] and held independent ideas about religion that he kept to himself. A public break with the Church resulted from an event that occurred when he was 52. By then, Voltaire was internationally known as a preeminent philosopher and had just spent a couple of years in the court of Frederick the Great in Potsdam.

He was on the road, returning to France from Prussia, when he received word that he had been expelled from France and could not enter the country. Earlier he'd published his masterpiece and the first-ever history of philosophy: *Essay of the Morals and the Spirit of the Nations from Charlemagne to Louis XIII.* The book traced the natural causation of the European mind and described the influences of various religions on European history, including Catholicism, Judaism, Islam, and even some Eastern religions.

His scholarly treatment of the subject was much too clinical for the Catholic Church. It felt that he seemed to imply there was no notable difference in validity among these various religions. Voltaire was forced into exile, and after that his writings became increasingly antiestablishment and increasingly critical of the Catholic Church, which remained the state religion of France even after the Reformation. But because of his wide literary following and reputation as the greatest intellect in Europe, the Church became desperate to regain his allegiance. In a remarkable attempt to buy his silence, they even offered him a position as Cardinal in the French Catholic Church. He refused.

Finally, at 83, after 26 years of exile, he was allowed to return to Paris. Hundreds of visitors requested an audience, including our Benjamin Franklin. As Voltaire grew increasingly ill, he faced an end-of-life dilemma between his personal belief

---

38   Jean Jacques Rousseau (1712–1778) was one of the first influential philosophers to reject institutionalized religions entirely. His belief in the goodness of God was a "new religion of the heart," neither Calvinist nor Catholic, but the heritage of everyone. His books were publicly burned in France. Nevertheless, his writings (excerpted and published outside France) had a strong influence on future leaders of the French Revolution, such as Robespierre. So much so that for a brief period around 1794 the official state religion of France—called the "Cult of the Supreme Being"—was inspired by Book IV of Rousseau's *Emile* (1762). *Emile* was also to play a crucial role in the development of the philosophy of Immanuel Kant.

about God and that of the Church. An abbé was sent to hear his final confession but was instructed to deny absolution unless Voltaire would sign a document attesting to his faith in orthodox Catholicism. Again he refused,[39] and the Church reacted by banning his burial in sacred ground. Friends, however, spirited his body out of Paris to a final resting place in sacred ground in Champagne, about a hundred miles to the east. The leaders of the French Revolution had his remains exhumed and brought back to Paris thirteen years later to be enshrined in the Panthéon.

Voltaire was influenced by Hinduism and Buddhism and tells the story of the "Good Brahmin" who speaks to the narrator thusly:

> "I have been studying these forty years, and I find that it is so much time lost. . . . I talk a great deal, and when I have done speaking, I remain confounded of what I have said." The same day I [the narrator] had a conversation with an old woman, his neighbor. I ask if she had ever been unhappy for not understanding how her soul was made. She had not, for the briefest moment of her life, had a thought about these subjects with which the good Brahmin had so tormented himself. She believed in the bottom of her heart in the metamorphoses of Vishnu, and provided she could get some of the sacred water of the Ganges in which to make her absolutions, she thought herself the happiest of women. Struck with the happiness of this poor creature, I returned to my philosopher, whom I thus addressed:
>
> "Are you not ashamed to be miserable when, not fifty yards from you, there is an old automaton who thinks of nothing and lives contented?"
>
> "You are right," he replied, "I have said to myself a thousand times that I should be happy if I were but as happy as my old neighbor; and yet it is a happiness that I do not desire."

---

39   Voltaire was not without a sense of humor. When pressed to condemn the devil before he died, Voltaire argued: "This is no time to make new enemies."

Voltaire not only became skeptical about Church dogma as he grew older but also about grand metaphysics as illustrated in the story of the Good Brahmin. His interest shifted from finding the Truth to finding what works for the most people. As his own belief in an afterlife weakened, he came to the view that even so, a heaven and hell for the soul was still necessary to the Christianity of the common man.[40]

Asked if he thought a group of atheists could operate as a moral society, Voltaire replied, "Yes, if they were also philosophers." Since few of us are philosophers, society needs the belief in an immortality of punishment or reward to restrain man's inhumanity to man. He felt that despite the Inquisition and other failings of the Church, including its treatment of him, it was more a force for good than evil in the world. And it was certainly better than the alternative of widespread superstition.

I begin to put more store on happiness and life than on truth.

—Voltaire

---

40   Belief that the common man needed Christianity was also true for our next philosopher, Immanuel Kant. He has been accused, half-jokingly, of finding a place for Christianity in his philosophy only out of compassion for his devout servant of forty years, Martin Lampe.

CHAPTER 7

PHILOSOPHY MATURES

Human reason has this particular fate, that in one species of its
knowledge it is burdened by questions . . . it is not able to ignore, but
which as transcending all its powers, it is also not able to answer.

—Immanuel Kant
The Critique of Pure Reason (1781)

THE GREAT GERMAN PHILOSOPHERS: KANT AND SCHOPENHAUER

KANT (1724–1804)

Immanuel Kant was born in Königsberg, Prussia, and into a different world than Voltaire. The pendulum had swung much further away from the use of religion to answer life's questions and towards the use of reason, especially in non-Catholic countries like Prussia. In fact, the late 1700s came to be known as the Age of Reason. Perhaps the most representative proponent of this practical view of the world was the historian and philosopher David Hume (1711–1776). He wrote that there was no soul, no mind, only perceptions. What we call mind was a string of perceptions organized as ideas. We inferred causes as a way of organizing our perceptions, but these were basically mere guesstimates as to their sources. There were no universal truths like Spinoza's ideas of substance. What was real was limited to mathematics and what could be concluded from scientifically documented observation. Religion, metaphysics, and other inferred general laws of nature, fell in the realm of "sophistry and illusion."

Kant was immersed in the high philosophical skepticism of his day, spending most of his life beginning at age sixteen as a student and later as a philosophy lecturer at the University of Königsberg, retiring at age seventy-two.[41] But, he wasn't entirely comfortable with the idea that there was nothing of truth in religion and metaphysics. Rousseau's *Emile* (1762) finally opened a door for him. Rousseau had argued that, while reason might correctly conclude that God and immortality of the soul were irrational and unproven beliefs—nevertheless, humanity overwhelmingly believed in them. Unless one felt compelled to give reason, and only reason, the ultimate authority over matters of truth, then who's to say humanity's intuition was not right in this case? Especially, Kant thought, if it could be demonstrated that the reasoning faculty itself had limitations that would cause it to be blind to some areas of reality.

Europe finally produced in Kant's classic, *The Critique of Pure Reason* (1781), a philosophical work rivaling Plato's *Republic* in importance, if not in readability. In the prevailing wisdom of the day, as championed by David Hume and John Locke, all our accumulated knowledge begins exclusively with observations and experimentation, with the limited exception of pure math. Kant argued that there must be other forces at work, not perceived and not dependent on observation. In *The Critique of Pure Reason* he illustrated how

---

41   The German population of Königsberg in East Prussia was expelled by the Soviets after World War II, and the University was converted to a Russian-speaking "Kaliningrad State University." But, in reverence to a higher-than-political value, it was renamed the "Immanuel Kant State University of Russia" in honor of Kant in the year 2005 in a ceremony attended by Russian President Vladimir Putin. (Wikipedia)

our minds are bombarded with countless sensations of sight, sound, touch, and taste. Raw sensations are flashing lights on the base of our eyes or static on our eardrums. They must be organized as to causality for us to be able to rank their importance. Our minds, *a priori*, have the ability to assign time and space to sensations because no experience would be possible to perceive without giving it a time and place. Perceptions, in turn, are ordered into conceptions by our innate template of cause, unity, and necessity. In other words, our mind isn't passive clay molded by the daily bombardment of sensations, but rather is already organized to process experience into a form useful to our survival. And these templates of organization in our minds existed before our first experience.

The key conclusions that Kant developed in 800 pages of the *Critique* was that our minds were more than just the passive results of experience and that there were limits on what we could truly know through reasoning. For example, concepts like time and space are useful tools for organizing sensory inputs, but they are just mental constructs, in other words, not real.[42] Therefore, what is truly out there will be presented to us through the screen of imagined time and space, whether we want it thus or not.

Ideas about religion, metaphysics, and transcendence belong in the world of *noumenon*,[43] that is, things that are implied by what we know from the world of phenomenon or appearances but are not knowable in the way we normally know things. They are not only outside our powers of perception, the way ultraviolent light is, but also outside our powers of conception. To Rousseau's original question, though, of whether reason should be the final arbiter of

---

42   I found an illustration from *Understanding the Great Philosophers*, by Henry Thomas, particularly helpful in understanding the "unreality" of our concept of time. Imagine you are flying (commercially) from Washington to New York with a layover in Philadelphia. For you—as you sit on your layover in the Philadelphia airport—Washington was, Philadelphia is, and New York will be. But, in reality, Washington is, Philadelphia is, and New York is. As an aside, Albert Einstein, more than a century later, acknowledged the early influence of *The Critique* on his Theory of Relativity, particularly on the relativity of time in our consciousness.

43   "A posited object or event as it appears in itself independent of perception by the senses." *Merriam-Webster's Collegiate Dictionary*, Eleventh Edition.

the existence of the religious or the transcendent, Kant would say no. Reason doesn't have the wherewithal to say yes or no on questions of noumenon. Perhaps it's better to rely on faith. "I believe in order to understand," said St. Anselm, Archbishop of Canterbury (circa 1077 CE).

These innate agents for organizing perceptual input may place limits on the ultimate range of our knowledge, but we shouldn't overlook their positive contributions in helping us to survive as a species, thus far. Nevertheless, Kant went on to show that the limits of cognitive ability go beyond just the inability to know ultimate reality. We can't even know everyday, common phenomena, like trees. We may have detailed knowledge about how they appear to us with various measurements and descriptions of physical attributes as well as information on how they affect us emotionally. The object itself is transformed into our idea of what it is. But what was it before being so transformed? We do not know. The object is but a mirror, reflecting what we see and think it is. We really don't know what's behind the mirror: what the "thing-in-itself" is. As Schopenhauer later said, "Kant's greatest merit is the distinction of the phenomenon from the thing-in-itself. . . . Understanding can never go beyond the limits of our sensibility." Anaïs Nin expressed it differently: "We don't see things as they are; we see them as we are."

Kant's new book made its way slowly around the intelligentsia of Europe. Many professed an inability to understand it. But gradually, those who did understand it were convinced he was right in his revolutionary theory of cognition. This was a decided setback to those who believed in the ultimate power of reason to understanding our total world, as well as to those idealists who believed that we could eventually prove the truth of religion or metaphysics. But, like the "Good Brahmin" in Voltaire's tale, there were many who would not accept the notion that simple religious faith was the only possible path to universal truth. Those longing for a metaphysical path would seek a way around Kant's obstruction like water around a logjam. Kant does not say that knowledge about the thing-in-itself or some ultimate truth does not exist, but he does end the notion that reason would eventually reveal what it is. But what other way is there?

The weakness of Kant's writing was its obtuseness. He was once asked why he never used examples to illustrate his points. He answered that he had considered using examples but decided they would make *The Critique of Pure Reason* too long, since it was already 800 pages sans examples. Herbert Spencer, who was referred to earlier as having rejected Plato's *Republic* as nonsense, admitted he couldn't understand Kant's writings. Nevertheless, *The Critique* was proclaimed a monumental achievement by intellectuals, probably including a significant number who didn't understand it or hadn't even read it thoroughly.[44] Because of the obtuseness—also the potential for multiple interpretations of Kant's philosophy—a number of philosophers rose to prominence by claiming they truly understood Kant, and then they layered on top their own turgid philosophy. Not many in the academic community were willing to risk their reputation by challenging these renowned post-Kant philosophers—because that would involve, first, really understanding Kant and, second, embarking on the arduous work of digging through many levels of arcane pronouncements from these self-proclaimed Kantian "disciples." Hegel, Schilling, and Fichte were all well-respected philosophers of the early nineteenth century who claimed to be heirs of Kant. By various methods they offered a way around the supposed impossibility of reasoning one's way to ultimate truth.

One philosopher did take on the challenge of debunking them. Schopenhauer tried[45]—unsuccessfully in his lifetime—to convince people that these pseudo-Kantians merely substituted some form of the concept of "understanding" for that of "reason," and then proceeded to draw whatever

---

44   I have never attempted to read *The Critique of Pure Reason*, on the advice of those who have. My secondhand interpretations could, therefore, be considered suspect.

45   Schopenhauer, in his attempt to refute Hegel's interpretation of Kant, actually scheduled his lectures on the subject at the very same time as Hegel's at the University of Berlin. This was a complete failure, leaving Schopenhauer to lecture to virtually empty classrooms.

conclusions they preferred, all the while claiming to be followers of Kant. Later revisionists of history would side with Schopenhauer.[46]

Kant's writings had a profound impact on theologians, too. The Roman Catholic Church had heretofore attracted religious intellectuals who appreciated the magnificent achievements of the ancient Greek philosophers—not so much for their metaphysics, which could quickly turn heretical—but for their development of the art of logical argument. Some of these intellectuals achieved great fame using logical gymnastics to prove Christian theology was based on reason as well as on faith. Though Kant didn't close the door on faith, he did close it on logical reasoning as a way of proving the existence of God. His work showed that the famous Catholic logicians, like Thomas Aquinas, were essentially apologists—presumably motivated by their sincere faith.

We began this path through philosophy with a search for the experience of transcendence under the more common meaning of the term; that is, going beyond our normal, everyday state of being or experience. Kant was the first to use the term, "transcendental philosophy," which had a special meaning: He was referring to concepts about those areas of our cognition that aid us in our perception of phenomena but are *a priori* and hidden. In other words, we can entertain a philosophy about these areas, but this philosophy is transcendental since it goes beyond anything we can know or prove. He also used a different term, "transcendent," to refer to all the reality that is beyond the limits of our powers of cognition. As to how to speculate about this transcendent reality, he could only suggest the practice of faith. This tedious discussion of terminology is introduced here because a very significant development took

---

46 "Not very long ago it was the custom for historians of philosophy to give the immediate successors of Kant—to Fichte, Schilling, and Hegel . . . much honor. . . . Our perspective today is a little different, and we enjoy perhaps too keenly the invective leveled by Schopenhauer. . . . By reading Kant, said Schopenhauer, 'the public was compelled to see that what is obscure is not always without significance.' Fichte and Schilling took advantage of this and excogitated magnificent spider-webs of metaphysics. 'But the height of audacity in serving up pure nonsense . . . was finally reached in Hegel.'" Will Durant, *The Story of Philosophy* (1926, p. 130).

place in America, called the "Transcendentalist Movement," based to some degree on Kant's writings. This movement, as well as its luminaries, Emerson and Thoreau, will be discussed later.

If we began our search for transcendence in philosophy with the Platonic idealism of finding knowledge of the sublime through philosophic discourse and reasoning, Kant has set us straight. The good news is that he believed that a transcendent, non-rational world does exist, without which there would be no phenomenal world. For example, without the *a priori* and unseen mental constructs of time and space, we could not comprehend what we see. The bad news for Platonic idealism is that the human reasoning faculty was not designed to comprehend this transcendent world and possibly never will.

Is there another way? We're not done with philosophy yet.

SCHOPENHAUER (1788–1860)

There is no philosopher for whom the disparity between influence and academic reputation is as great as it is for Schopenhauer. . . . It is nonetheless striking that many of the founders of modernity in its contemporary guise, from Wagner in music, and Mann and Proust in literature to Nietzsche and Wittgenstein in philosophy to Freud in psychiatry, owe their deepest intellectual debts to Schopenhauer or, in Freud's case, found themselves uncannily anticipated by him.[47]

Arthur Schopenhauer's lack of academic reputation owed much to his insufferable personality: he was not a man one would want to know personally.

---

47   Robert Retry, contributor to *A Companion to Continental Philosophy*, edited by Simon Critchley and William R. Schroeder (1998, p. 149). Mr. Retry cites and documents many examples of how Schopenhauer directly influenced these "founders of modernity."
Thomas Mann in his essay "Schopenhauer" (1938), reminded Sigmund Freud that his concept of the "id" and "ego" directly corresponded to Schopenhauer's "will" and "intellect," as did the dominance he gave to the sexual drive in influencing human behavior.

His mother threw him out; he denied responsibility for his illegitimate only child; he hated women and Jews; was dismissive of the academic philosophy establishment; slept next to a loaded pistol; and couldn't live under the same roof with anyone. Even those who could ignore these shortcomings were forced to endure the pervasive pessimism of his writings. Yet, in some areas he spoke clearly, passionately, and convincingly. He seemed to revel in erecting horrific barriers to public acceptance, totally convinced that the pure truth of his ideas would one day conquer all.

One was lucky in one way to be a philosopher after Kant. He saved those who followed him much wasted effort. He had demonstrated the limits of the philosophical materialism of Bacon, Hume, and Locke by demonstrating there was reality beyond the power of the senses to know empirically. The idealists, like Socrates and Plato, understood this, but Kant also destroyed their notion that one could ever reason one's way to knowledge of this transcendent reality.

We know an object by its material composition within our cognitive constraints of time, space, and estimated cause. That's all we can know. But what about the part implied, that thing-in-itself, where reasoning can never take us? Kant left one door open. "[T]he something that underlies outward phenomenon might possibly . . . be the subject of ideas at the same time." That was enough for Hegel, Schilling, and Fichte to run with and use reasoning to identify the thing-in-itself, despite Kant's conclusion that it lay outside reason.

Schopenhauer's approach, on the other hand, was to accept Kant's conclusion that reasoning—the typical academic approach—was not the way to know the other side of appearance. His eureka moment was to intuit the answer: *direct experience is not the same as reason*, a startlingly simple but profound missing piece of the puzzle. We could never know the thing-in-itself of a tree, but we do have direct, bodily knowledge of ourselves that is hidden to others. We see both sides of our own mirror. And perhaps we can infer from our case what the other side of the mirror looks like for others.

But it is only on my body that I am, and simultaneously feel, that which I can explain in the act of representation. I can transfer myself into the world of objects and yet simultaneously, I am the 'thing-in-itself.' Self-expression of my body is the only point at which I can discover what the world is apart from my representation. The double knowledge we have of nature and action of our own body, and which is given in two different ways . . . we shall use . . . as a key to the inner being of every phenomenon in nature. We shall judge all objects which are not our own body, and therefore are given to our consciousness not in a double way but only as representation. . . . We shall therefore assume that as, on one hand, they are representations, just as our body, and are in this respect homogeneous with it, so on the other hand, if we set aside their existence, as the subject's representation, what shall remain over must be, according to its inner nature, the same as what in ourselves we call will. For what other source could we take the elements out of which we construct such a world? Besides the will and the representation, there is absolutely nothing known or conceivable. (WWR I, p. 104–5)

There you have it! Modern Western philosophy wrapped up in Schopenhauer's masterpiece, *The World as Will and Representation* (WWR I), begun when he was age twenty-six and published four years later in 1818. Upon publication he declared that the Sphinx,[48] to keep her honor, should throw herself into the abyss as she swore to do once her riddles were solved. But the public response was underwhelming: the books sat on store shelves, and sat and sat. When the publisher refused to publish a second edition

---

48   Sphinx. She was a monster from ancient Greek mythology who had the head of a woman, body of a lioness, wings of an eagle, and tail of a serpent. She waited outside Thebes to devour travelers who could not solve her riddles. When Oedipus correctly answered her riddle, she reportedly threw herself off a cliff and died.

(WWR II) seventeen years later, Schopenhauer had to pay the publishing costs. But luckily, he had inherited wealth and did not need to earn a living as a professional philosopher. It would still take another twenty years after that for his genius to be recognized.

Let's return to the main theme of his book. We begin with Schopenhauer's revelation that we can only experience Kant's thing-in-itself in our own body. But why call that experience "will"? The term does not mean what it normally means to others, or what could be called "free will." "I will go downtown," or "my willpower kept me from eating that rich dessert," and so forth. Schopenhauer's "will" is the virtually the opposite: unconscious motivation outside our control. He makes a distinction between "our will" and "the will."

The will that is imparted to us at birth is a survival guide, benefitting the species, and remaining largely unconscious.[49] For example, you don't decide to trigger the fight-or-flight syndrome—your body does. The will's purpose is to insure the physical survival of the individual, at least long enough to procreate and to protect his or her young, thereby insuring the species' survival. An example of one of our innate survival instincts is hoarding or saving as security against unpredictable hard times that might otherwise imperil a family's survival. An easy way to visualize the byproduct of this hoarding is the buildup of body fat in good times to draw on during famine. However, when resources are limited, hoarding leads to competition, aggression, and war. A final legacy of the species' will is the general desire for sensual pleasure and avoidance of pain, the "carrot and stick" approach to motivating behavior aligned with the goals of the species.

---

49 "It is the dark, inaccessible part of our personality. . . . [W]e all approach the id [unconscious will] with analogies: we call it chaos, a cauldron full of seething excitations. . . . It is filled with energy reaching it from the instincts, but it has no organization, produces no collective will, but only a striving to bring about the instinctual needs." Sigmund Freud, "New Introductory Lectures in Psychoanalysis," 1933.

At the bottom of all things, there is only one identical force, always equal and ever the same, which slumbers in plants, awakens in animals, but finds consciousness only in man—the WILL.

—Ralph Waldo Emerson
JMN, vol. 15, 1860–1866

In animals, unconscious will or instinct is sufficient. But, man needs reasons for what he wants, resulting in philosophies for why he wants what he wants. These rationalizations produce illusions like concepts of individual determinism and strong free will. Referring to our intellect, Schopenhauer says, "Man has produced it for the service of the individual will." Whereas the reasoning of the intellect is modified from time to time, "The will is the only permanent and unchangeable element in the mind," he adds. But the intellect still plays an essential role in survival, even as it services the will. The intellect is the basis of man's sentience, reasoning, and language. The enormous problem-solving ability it possesses ensures no other species can seriously threaten us, if we don't destroy ourselves first.

Schopenhauer argues that self-awareness allows us, at least briefly, to notice and be aware of the omnipresent will, the incessant chatter in our heads instructing us to do this or that. Meanwhile, unconscious primal urges, such as eating, having sex, or running in fear, can produce chemical reactions in our bodies. At high-enough levels, these will simply brush aside conscious reasoning. Later we can lament or rationalize why we did what we did.

For example, Schopenhauer was driven into deep melancholy over his inability to control his sexual urges. These desires and urgings of the will arise spontaneously, without any help from our intellect. They exist before we think. Schopenhauer did not deny the existence of some independent free will. But, like Spinoza, he believed that this free will was limited, and that the vast majority of humans seriously underestimated the part the unconscious will of the species played in everyday decisions and actions.

Schopenhauer's pessimism was born in a pessimistic time in European history. The prior period, called the Enlightenment, was relatively optimistic. Rapid progress in the practical sciences had improved the material life of millions, and the future held promise for even more dramatic improvements. Some monarchies had shown a willingness to share power peacefully with the emerging middle class. The egalitarian ideals of the American and French revolutions were leading to more humane societies with less class distinction. All that would change. The pivotal event came in 1803, when Napoleon high-jacked the French Revolution and crowned himself Emperor. To Schopenhauer, Napoleon was proof positive of the negative potential of will unchecked by normal social constraints. Here was a man with a once-in-a-lifetime combination of charisma and cunning, appearing at just the right time, capturing virtually exclusive control of perhaps the most powerful nation on earth. In France, his will was law; but even France was not enough. Before Napoleon's will could be arrested and contained to St. Helena, Europe had been devastated. Millions lay dead, and there was economic depression everywhere. The humanistic ideals of the Enlightenment and the French Revolution were rolled back, and many of the exclusive privileges of the aristocracy were re-established.

In his youth, Schopenhauer had no place for religion, which he called "the metaphysics of the masses." Later in life, he began to realize the potential of religion in helping to control the negative influence of unbridled will. He felt Christianity had a role to play since it taught the doctrine of original sin, which he equated to individual blind will, and the doctrine of salvation through the denial of some of our desires. He also thought Buddhism was a purer confirmation of his beliefs since, as he saw it, total dominance over our will was the essential doctrine of the religion.

He believed our intellect was designed as a servant of the will. Basically, it has given us tools that augment our instinctual survival skills. It was not designed, however, to contemplate sublimity. As the Borg on the television series, "Star Trek, The Next Generation," could conceivably say: "Sublimity is irrelevant" to survival. But, as sentient beings, we can't help wondering about the existence of an unseen reality, even though—with our limited cognitive abilities—we couldn't recognize it if we saw it. *Perhaps, though, we can experience it the way our body experiences things and thereby transcend our cognitive boundaries.* Ideas like these, under his term, "better consciousness," came to a younger, more optimistic, Schopenhauer. Could we call this "transcendence?"

> When some external cause or inward disposition lifts us suddenly out of the endless stream of willing, and delivers knowledge out of the slavery of the will, the attention is no longer directed to the motives of willing, but comprehends things free of their relationship to the will, and thus observes them without personal interest, without subjectivity, purely objectively[50]—gives itself entirely up to them as far as they are ideas, but not so far as they are motives. *Then all at once the peace which we were always seeking, but which always fled from us on the former path of the desires, comes to us on its own accord, and it is well with us.* It is the painless state which Epicurus prized as the highest good and the state of the gods; for we are for the moment set free from the miserable stirrings of the will; we keep the Sabbath of the penal servitude of willing; and the wheel of Ixion stands still. (*WWR* 1, p. 254 [emphasis mine].)

Schopenhauer experienced a few moments of better consciousness climbing Mount Schneekoppe in Bavaria in 1804 at age sixteen, on a tour of Europe with his parents. He began the climb in pre-dawn, and when he reached the

---

50   "He [Schopenhauer] was already in the light [top of Mount Schneekoppe] while down below darkness still reigned. 'One sees the world in chaos below one.' On top, however, all is of incisive clarity. And when the sun finally lights up the valley, it does not discover there smiling, delightful plains but offers to the gaze 'the eternal alteration of mountains and valleys, forests and meadows and towns and villages.'"Rüdiger Safranski, *Schopenhauer and the Wild Years of Philosophy*, (1991. p. 51)

peak, his senses were confounded by the contrast of sunlight dawning on the peak while the rest of Bavaria below him was still bathed in the dark of night. Philosophical clarity above and ignorance below.

For a few moments he found "the peace for which we were always seeking." He was so moved that he uncharacteristically played the role of common tourist by signing the climber's comment ledger on his return to the base of the hill:

> *Who can climb*
> *And remain silent?*
>
> —Arthur Schopenhauer from Hamburg

As Schopenhauer's philosophy matured, he searched for a way to describe better consciousness, knowing that language was not up to the task. "[W]hat we cannot talk about we must pass over in silence."[51] He experimented with imagery to come as close as possible to conveying in language his meaning of escaping "the endless stream of willing." He used the image of a sphere in which existed the state of non-willing. When you have suffered greatly, you may become so disillusioned with life to find yourself up against this sphere, feeling that if you could only enter, you would be rid of your suffering. But efforts to enter the sphere only put you in motion around it. After a period of trying, you stop, and are drawn slowly back into your old workaday world, striving again for the ends that will never satisfy.

There could be endless speculation as to what lay within that sphere, but Schopenhauer felt that whatever it was, language was not up to the task of describing it. Language and philosophy could bring you to the sphere but could not tell you how to enter. Schopenhauer never claimed that he had

---

51   "The whole sense of this book might be summed up in the following words: What can be said at all can be said clearly and what we cannot talk about we must pass over in silence." [Italics mine.] Ludwig Wittgenstein, *Tractatus Logico-Philosophicus*, 1921.

arrived at that will-less state, except for brief moments, such as at the peak of Mount Schneekoppe.

When I began my search for transcendence through philosophy, I envisioned that the end—if it lay within philosophy—would be reached according to the Platonic ideal of studying at the feet of the great philosophers of history. This book has followed the normal academic pattern of study and reason that hopefully progresses upwards to higher and higher truths. But with Kant and Schopenhauer we come to the realization that study and reason, because of the inherent limits of our cognition, will never carry us across the threshold of transcendence. *But, on the other hand, these philosophers do convey quite clearly that a transcendent reality does, in fact, exist.*

TRANSCENDENTALISM

No review of philosophy would be complete if we didn't address transcendentalism, especially since our motivation is the search for transcendence. We could call this a side road because it was more of a movement than a philosophy—and, unlike Schopenhauer, didn't really add anything new to the work of Kant. The movement is significant, though, as a manifestation of the importance that a philosophy like Kant's can have in the world of action.

If there were ever a meritorious intellectual aristocracy in America—harking back to Athens in the 400s BCE—it existed in and around Concord, Massachusetts, for three decades (1830–1860). Almost all of this aristocracy belonged to an informal group called the Transcendental Club, founded in 1836. "There was no club in the strict sense . . . only occasional meetings of like-minded men and women," wrote Henry Hedge, one of the original members. But those "like-minded men and women" read like a "Who's Who" of the framers of 19th-century American thought:

- Ralph Waldo Emerson—Foremost American philosopher
- Henry David Thoreau—Individualist & naturalist
- William Ellery Channing—Congregationalist, later founder of Unitarianism
- Theodore Parker—Co-founder of new Unitarian religion
- Amos Bronson Alcott—Education reformer; father of Louisa May Alcott
- Margaret Fuller—Pioneer for women's rights

Emerson's philosophy rejected the rationalism of John Locke and David Hume, and found agreement with Kant's method of reconciling materialism and idealism. Materialism belonged in the knowable world of phenomena, and idealism in the unknowable world of noumena. Kant named "all knowledge *transcendental* which is concerned not with objects but with our mode of knowing objects." [Italics mine.] He also called the self "a transcendental unity of the apperception"—in other words, introspective self-consciousness. Emerson saw this as a new way of viewing the self that was not limited by materialism and allowed for immaterial values that transcended our sensual perceptions.

Kant's writings provided the philosophical base and led to the naming of the movement called transcendentalism, but much more was tacked on by Emerson and others. Kant's concept of the self was too abstract and did not offer any guidance to action. Drawing on the writings of English humanists, German idealists, Christian mystics, and Eastern religions, the Club developed—but did not publish[52]—their meaning of tanscendentalism:

---

52   Not finding an existing publisher willing to print their thoughts, the Transcendentalists decided to produce their own periodical, *The Dial*. Margret Fuller was the main editor and George Ripley the managing editor (later to gain fame as the founder of the short-lived Transcendentalist utopian experiment at Brook Farm in the mid–1840s that attracted many New England intellectuals such as Nathaniel Hawthorne). With only two hundred subscribers the publication was not financially viable and ceased publication in 1844. Horace Greeley reported it as an end to the "most original and thoughtful periodical ever published in this country."

[I]ts proponents emphasized the divine in nature, the value of the individual and of human intuition, and a spiritual reality that 'transcends' sensory experience, while also providing a better guide for life than purely empirical or logical reasoning. The term refers to a cluster of concepts set forth by a number of individuals rather than a formal philosophy.

—Ashton Nichols, Professor of English, Dickinson College
Emerson, Thoreau, and the Transcendentalist Movement
The Teaching Company (2006)

Although transcendentalism was a conglomeration of philosophies, religions, and other sources, it did create strong motivation that led to value-based action. Thoreau's *Civil Disobedience* inspired Mahatma Gandhi and Martin Luther King, and, of course, his tale of Walden Pond has inspired naturalists and meditation enthusiasts to this day. Frederick Douglas, Emily Dickinson, John Brown, Louisa May Alcott, and Walt Whitman knew and were inspired by the Transcendentalists. Amos Bronson Alcott helped transform the form of education in America from a boot-camp mentality to one recognizing the uniqueness of the individual student and encouraging his or her participation in classroom discussion. Susan B. Anthony said Margaret Fuller "possessed more influence on the thought of American women than any woman prior to her time."

As an organized movement, transcendentalism faded from the scene in the second half of the nineteenth century; some date the end around 1860, others at Emerson's death in 1888. My guess is that it was eventually overwhelmed, as a broad movement, by modern commercialism. Of course, Unitarianism as a religion still exists today. Religions seem to have longer life spans than philosophies. I believe one message for us is that a useful philosophy, even one based on an individual's inward contemplation, must eventually return to value-based action in the community to be complete. The transcendentalists gave us the nonpareil example of this process.

Thoreau described in *Walden* personal transcendent experiences similar to the ones in the beginning of this book, and we will return to him later. We will end this discussion of Transcendentalism with an experience related by Emerson in his "Nature" essay (1836):

> Standing on the bare ground,—my head bathed by the blithe air, and uplifted into infinite space,—all mean egotism vanishes. I become a transparent eye-ball; I am nothing; I see all; the currents of the Universal Being circulate through me. I am part or particle of God.

NIETZSCHE (1844–1900)

Frederick Wilhelm Nietzsche, a gifted scholar of ancient Greece, was at one time considered a disciple of Schopenhauer and followed a natural progression of thought from Kant through Schopenhauer to him. Then something changed. Henry Thomas[53] dates the change around 1868, when Nietzsche was discharged from the army, unable to endure the physical challenges of a military life. Freed from actually having to live that kind of life, he was inspired to glorify it. He turned Schopenhauer's *The World As Will and Representation* upside down. Instead of condemning the tendency of the will toward aggression, he embraced it.

> I felt for the first time that the highest Will to Life does not find expression in a miserable struggle for existence, but in a Will to Power, a Will to Overcome, a Will to War.[54]

---

53   Henry Thomas, Ph.D., *Understanding the Great Philosophers* (UGP, 1962, p. 284).

54   Förster-Nietzsche, "The Young Nietzsche," London (1912, p. 235)

The will to kill for conquest and subjugation, throwing off the shackles of Christianity and democracy, was his suggested path to transcendence. He named his transcendent individual Übermensch (Superman). And he believed Napoleon[55] embodied that ideal.

> And thus the young disciple of Schopenhauer began to distort his master's teaching. Schopenhauer said that our aggressiveness, the will to live, is the greatest misfortune of the world. But Nietzsche declared this aggressiveness, the will to kill in order to live, is the noblest objective in the world.
>
> —Henry Thomas (UGP, p.284)

Although he was not actually committed to an insane asylum until age forty-five, Nietzsche's slide into madness probably progressed over a great many years before then. His version of Plato's Philosopher-King was a Superman "Blond Beast" whose mission was to rescue the elite from the "democrats, the Christians, and the cows." The "cows" were the herd of slave-like beings who made up the mediocrity, that is, common man. Their sole meaning should be service to the Blond Beast and the elite. (UGP, p. 289)

> Yet I think no one who lived in the Third Reich could have failed to be impressed by Nietzsche's influence on it. . . . Nazi scribblers never tired of extolling him. Hitler often visited the Nietzsche museum in Weimar and publicized his veneration for the philosopher by posing photographs of himself staring in rapture at the bust of the great man. . . . Finally there was Nietzsche's prophecy of the coming elite who would rule the world and from whom the superman would spring.

---

55 "It is to Napoleon that the honor will one day be given for having made for a time in which the man, the warrior, outweighed the tradesman and the Philistine." Frederick Wilhelm Nietzsche, *The Gay Science* (1910).

In *The Will to Power* he exclaims: "A daring and ruler race is building itself up. . . . The aim should be to prepare a transvaluation of values for a particularly strong kind of man, most highly gifted in intellect and will. This man and the elite around him will become the "lords of the earth." . . . "Lords of the Earth"[56] is a familiar expression in *Mein Kampf.* That in the end Hitler considered himself the superman of Nietzsche's prophecy cannot be doubted."

—William L. Shirer
The Rise and Fall of the Third Reich, 1960, p. 100–101.

Imagine the following scene. In 1938 amidst the snowy peaks of the Brenner Pass in the Alps, where the "Pact of Steel" between Germany and Italy would be signed two years later, Adolf Hitler presents Benito Mussolini with a set of the complete works of Nietzsche because of their mutual love for the philosopher: the patron saint of dictators. Yet Schopenhauer is ignored, while academics apologize for Nietzsche, claiming that deists purposely misinterpret him. Why? Because of his famous "God is dead" statement. To me these seem like "straw man" arguments. His ranting about a blond "Superman" and his undeniable insanity do much more to impugn his philosophy in my opinion than his "God is dead" proclamation.

PHILOSOPHERS OTHER THAN NIETZSCHE

I believe we have come to the end of the train tracks with Kant-Schopenhauer. In other words, philosophers may be unable to take us any further toward transcendence given the limits of man's cognitive powers and language—with the exception of Schopenhauer's unfinished work on "better consciousness." We climb off the train of traditional philosophy and find an

---

56   This reminds me of the "lords of the universe" description of the mentality of "fat-cat" financiers on Wall Street who led this country into the Great Recession of 2008 to 2010.

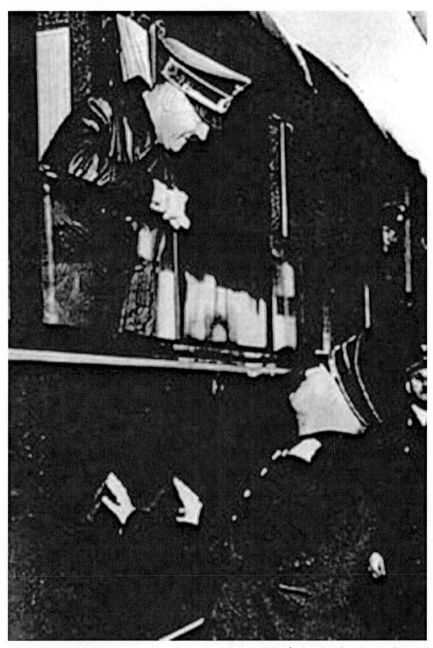

Brenner Pass: Hitler & Mussolini (http://ww2today.com/)

open field before us. A crowd has gathered, and some are taking tentative steps across the field. Philosophical guides have split into several schools such as the existential, analytical (neo-empirical), Marxist, Neo-Scholastic (Catholic), and others. There are none to follow, as far as I can determine, who are particularly interested in a metaphysical path, save perhaps Santayana. We should pay some attention to them, especially the Existentialists, but I don't want to interrupt the process here with more side roads in philosophy. So, I refer the reader to the Appendix: "Existentialism."

Kierkegaard, as one of the existential school, does make an interesting point worth addressing here in passing. He argues that despite the fact we cannot rationally know anything about the spiritual realm, and therefore have nothing to justify our choices, man still needs to have a spiritually inspired guide for his choices. Otherwise, his only guide is the dictates of the will. Like the sensualists in Plato's cave, he would be without an internal rudder and open to manipulation. Kierkegaard advocates that we stop trying to justify our choices with reason and make a simple "leap of faith" commitment. By his backhanded reasoning, religion is the best choice because it suggests upfront that one must eschew reason and rely totally on faith. Religion or not, it's important to commit, to establish our internal rudder, and then to take responsibility for our commitment. The psychiatrist Carl Jung called this commitment a "religious outlook."

> Among my patients in the second half of life—that is to say over thirty-five—there has not been one whose problem in the last resort was not that of finding a religious outlook on life. It is safe to say that every one of them fell ill because he had lost that which the living religions of every age have given to their followers, and none of them has truly been healed who did not regain his religious outlook.
>
> —Carl Jung
>
> *Psychology and Religion*, 1938

The religious folk, all along, have been suggesting we base our philosophy/ religion on faith.[57] But if our religion is inherited from our parents or comes by a leap of faith, are we taking responsibility for our choice? Can we truly call it our own? It would help if we could find something inside, unique to us, which would at least give us a hint of our authenticity—something along the lines of Schopenhauer's "better consciousness."

---

57   In my study of philosophy, I've often wondered why it lost out to religion in appealing to men's hearts. In Europe, Christianity swept away philosophy and various pagan religions in only a couple of centuries following Jesus's crucifixion. What was it at the core of this movement that gave it such power? It's hard to cut through all the manifestations of the religion today to find the answer. As best I can work out from my limited historical research, it was not the life and teachings of Jesus that ignited Christianity, but rather the way He left us. At the moment of Resurrection, there was a miraculous rip in the barrier that separated the divine from ordinary human existence. God allowed His power to flow into the realm of humans in the transfiguration of Jesus, and through Him to his followers. According to Paul, this could make forgiveness of sin and salvation a present reality for those willing to accept this gift. No more need to live a life of piety to earn salvation post-mortem. We all sin through our unkind words and deeds that injure God's creatures—a debt that we must repay. Jesus, though, paid our debt with his death on the cross. But, the Resurrection also brought new powers to early believers. They were powers to overcome many of man's most vexing problems, such as slavery, immoral desire, and even death. There were also new powers of rectitude and improved speech to help believers proselytize Christianity. Whether or not these powers were really divine, belief made them real. These Christians could endure even martyrdom, which they saw as only a stage in their new life leading to an early reunion with Christ.

CHAPTER 8

BETTER CONSCIOUSNESS

In starting to forge our own way forward, we can take a look at meditation,[58] with fresh input from Schopenhauer's concept of the will and better consciousness. His sphere of better consciousness could never be entered by reason or when the will was in conscious operation. But, "When some external cause or inward disposition lifts us suddenly out of the endless stream of willing. . . . Then all at once the peace which we were always seeking . . . comes to us on its own accord."

I believe he was referring to a transcendent event, like his reaching the peak of Mount Schneekoppe at sunrise, causing an unexpected reaction that suddenly overwhelmed his senses. These events are unplanned. In the meantime, what can we do to make us more open to such experiences?

---

58   Meditation's benefits are popularly associated with the "relaxation response," a beneficial mind-body state of deep relaxation, similar to sleep and popularized by a book of the same name by Dr. Herbert Benson, published in 1975. Dr. Benson, of Harvard Medical School, advocated a method of meditation based on the "Transcendental Meditation" technique, as taught by Maharishi Mahesh Yogi. (See the "Relaxation Response" website.)

MEDITATION

Consider a planned daily experience, that is certainly nonrational, called meditation—especially *zazen*, the Zen Buddhist version. In the practice of Zen, the hope is for "enlightenment."[59] But just the relief from the constant buzzing of the will, derived from the practice of *zazen* thirty minutes a day, can have beneficial effects. Even so, the will does intrude on meditation from time to time. Another avowed goal of the Zen approach is to alert us and make us aware—make us mindful—of the working of the will,[60] which is easier to notice during meditation. We have a chance to learn what Schopenhauer was talking about concerning the will.

Finally, there is the focus in *zazen* on the present moment, where the heart of Zen resides.

Each moment is all being, is the entire world.

Reflect now whether any being or any world is left out of the present moment.

—Dōgen (1200–1253)

---

59   I have experienced enlightenment! It was not in response to meditation but to something I read by my Zen instructor, Ken Walkama. In a play on words, he wrote: "We are not what we think." My response cannot be expressed in words, but it involved intuitively understanding and truly believing that my personal mistakes of the past had no actual current existence except as brain waves in my head. This resulted in a profound feeling of self-forgiveness. The euphoria lasted for a couple of weeks. I thought that with my new insight, I had bested my internal critic for good; but it fought its way back persistently. The will is with us always. This experience has been my one and only enlightenment in three years of Zen practice.

60   The Buddhists have a term, Tanhā, which I think is similar to Schopenhauer's will. Tanhā can loosely be translated as our innate thirst or craving, which along with ignorance, leads to our suffering. "The origin of Tanhā (craving, unwholesome desire, wish, thirst), extends beyond the desire for material objects or sense pleasures. It also includes the desire for life . . . the desire for fame." (*Wikipedia*).

As for advice on the actual practice of *zazen*, I would recommend *The Miracle of Mindfulness, An Introduction to the Practice of Meditation* (1975), by Thich Nhat Hanh. (Because of his tireless efforts to bring peace to his homeland of Vietnam, Mr. Hahn was recommended for the Nobel Peace prize by Martin Luther King, Jr., in 1967.) *Zazen* can be practiced alone anywhere, but group practice is more powerful. I think as Westerners without a meditation tradition, we respond to the confirmation from a group that what we're doing is OK. It's also hard to overestimate the benefits of what you can learn from the leader of the group, who is often willing to meet one-on-one to discuss Zen practice. In the last chapter, on a real-world practice of personal philosophy, I will return to this subject and making it part of daily life.

PEAK EXPERIENCES (EXPERIENCES "OF THE ORDER OF LIFE ITSELF")

If ever the passing moment is such that I wish it not to pass and say to it "You are so beautiful, stay awhile," then let that be the finish. . . . Dreaming of this incomparable moment, I now taste and enjoy the supreme moment.

—Johann Wolfgang von Goethe

Faust (1808)

[This passage refers to a suggestion by Faust to the devil, Mephistopheles, concerning the timing of the end of their bargain.]

There are ends in life, i.e., experiences which are so precious in themselves as to prove that not everything is a means to some end other than itself. (75)

—Abraham Maslow

We have now left philosophy and meditation and come to psychology. We jump almost to the present with the publication of *Religion, Values and Peak-Experiences* (1964) by Abraham Maslow (1908–1970), best known for his behavioral theory concerning the hierarchy of human needs. As a practicing psychologist, he grew weary of treating sick people who spent so much time obsessing about the negatives of life. He made a decision to reverse course and study well-adjusted people to learn what made their lives successful.

In his theory, we are motivated by a desire to move up a scale of progressively higher achievements, beginning with basic survival and security, then building greater self-esteem through successful personal and community relationships, and finally—for the well-adjusted person—to the ultimate goal of self-actualization or being our own man or woman. When we leave our parents and become self-supporting, our basic needs are the most critical. But as we gain more mastery of our environment, our attention shifts to social needs, and we worry less about survival. The highest goal, self-actualization, involves our desire to reach our full potential, achieve our destiny. This is also the most fulfilling of the goals on a deep personal basis.

Less well-known is that Maslow also wrote about another plane of human experience, separate from his hierarchy of psychological needs: "peak experiences," which were even more fulfilling than self-actualization. The problem with these experiences was that they were rare, therefore difficult to study, and almost impossible to reproduce.

So, what are these peak experiences? We began this book with a few examples, and added one from Schopenhauer and one from Emerson along the way. Peak experiences are difficult to analyze because they are transcendent, that is, beyond logic and reasoning. Maslow did do a series of interviews and over the years identified several common characteristics. He lists 25 in *Religion, Values and Peak-Experiences*. Here are five of them:

1. "Peak-experiences can make life worthwhile by their occasional occurrence. They give meaning to life itself. They prove it to be worthwhile."

2. "In the peak-experience there is a very characteristic disorientation in time, and space, or even the lack of time and space,"

3. "The world seen in peak-experiences is seen only as beautiful, good, desirable, worthwhile, etc. and is never experienced as evil or undesirable."

4. "In peak-experiences, such emotions as wonder, awe, reverence, humility, surrender, and even worship before the greatness of the experience is often reported."

5. "What has been called the 'unitive consciousness' is often given in peak-experiences. i.e., a sense of the sacred glimpsed <u>in</u> and <u>through</u> the particular instance of the momentary, the secular, the worldly."

The next logical question is "How common are these experiences?" There are problems finding general population studies that use the terminology of peak experiences. Imagine handing out questionnaires to thousands of people who have little concept of peak experiences or transcendence. They would have no idea what was being asked. The most comprehensive surveys (National Opinion Research Center's General Social Survey) have asked Americans if they have ever had an intense *religious* experience that "lifted them out of themselves." These repeated surveys, along with similar ones in Great Britain, have actually been fairly consistent, with about a third answering "yes." I like to believe that the real number for all peak experiences is really twice that high. For example, I have had three or four peak experiences, yet I wouldn't classify any of them as religious.

Abraham Maslow noted that when he tried eliciting examples of peak experiences, many subjects who didn't already know what he was talking about would just look blank. He realized that he was using "analytic, scientific" terminology about an essentially ineffable experience. When he substituted metaphorical and more poetic language, he was more likely to hit a responsive chord.

I finally fell into the habit of expecting everyone to have peak-experiences and of being rather surprised if I ran across someone who could recall none at all.

—Abraham Maslow (22)

WHAT MAKES PEAK EXPERIENCES IMPORTANT?

AUTHENTICITY: Marlow's subjects reported their experiences resonated with something deep inside them, and were "more real than real"—seemingly more true than what we normally think of as reality. By comparison, what we typically see or hear from others and the media is subject to manipulation. Even our emotions and nighttime dreams—including nightmares—are manifestations of the will. But peak experiences, according to those reporting them, come from a source deep within the individual and are to be trusted above all other sources. These experiences are *of the order of life itself.*[61] If you are looking for guidance in making your Kierkegaard "leap of faith" commitment in life, your peak experiences could be the place to start.

EVIDENCE OF A TRANSCENDENT REALITY: Scientists and other skeptics will respond that any conclusions about peak experiences cannot be proven scientifically. Rousseau and Kant argued that scientists may not

---

61   Blaise Pascal (1623–1692), the great French mathematician and scientist, provided a remarkable account of a religious peak experience for one who was previously known for his skepticism of theology and philosophy. This account of the experience is from *Irrational Man* (1958, p. 16) by William Barrett.
"He [Pascal] had had a religious experience, connected with what he thought was a miraculous recovery from an illness, and so overpowering had been the visitation that he wrote down a note about the experience and sewed it into his clothing, as if it were a secret he had to keep as close as possible to himself. Whatever we may think of the validity of such experiences, for Pascal himself this lightning from heaven needed no proofs: it was *of the order of life itself*, not of rational theology. His life thereafter turned round that single and shattering experience, and he dedicated that life to religion." [Italics mine.]

be the best final judges on spiritual matters. Perhaps, then, there is room for conclusions based on faith or instinct, rather than reason.

But, peak experiences are none of the above. They are not derived from reasoning, faith, or the will. They come unbidden, something apart. Whether they are part of a transcendent reality cannot be answered by the scientist or the philosopher, but only by the individual who has had the experience. For me, peak experiences are proof of a better and transcendent reality.

EVIDENCE OF THE IMPORTANCE OF THE INDIVIDUAL: Peak experiences suggest that you and I are part of something larger and more important than we can discern from our everyday living. This gives meaning to our unique existence, apart from our responsibilities to family, community, and the species. In other words, through them we can know that we are intrinsically necessary. As Maslow put it, "To say this in a negative way, I would guess that peak experiences help to prevent suicide." Or as The Talmud says: "To kill a human being is to destroy a world."

PERSONAL TRANSCENDENT PEAK EXPERIENCE

My most clearly peak experience happened about fifty years ago. I knew from the beginning how extraordinarily fortunate I was to have had the experience, that it would be one of the highlighted moments of my life, and that it was a gift rather than something earned. Trying to remember, after all these years, what message I was receiving at the time, I recall: "It doesn't matter." Whatever came before or will come in the future, "It doesn't matter" or "It's all right." In those actual moments, though, time seemed frozen. I do recall for several weeks feeling that the world was a good place, but even if at times it was not, I was OK with that, too. This experience was staged by an event that would ultimately stun my senses and would open up in me the possibility of this gift. The actual situation was my first military parachute jump. Poetry, I believe in this case, seems the best way to try to recapture my feelings at the time.

TRANSCENDENCE OVER GEORGIA

Two dozen hapless souls sit
contemplating their first step
into
   Georgia
      air.
The C-47 props continue their relentless throb.
In the dark hull, ghostly faces search inward for strength.
Just tell the sergeant—I implore myself—
"Today is not good for me. Tomorrow, maybe."
A light somewhere down the line.
No! The sergeant's shinning face adjacent an open door.
To keep my breakfast I look quickly to the floor.

Then the dreaded order comes,
"STAND UP!
Turn to the door!
(Clicking, stomping, boots as the move is executed.)
Sound-off:
Static line?" "OK!"
"Equipment check?" "OK!"
"GO! GO! GO!"

"GRRRR," comes the exaggerated airborne growl in unison
and forty-eight shuffling boots are set in motion
slamming wooden planking against the metal fuselage.

Wham! Wham! Wham! Deafening sound.
My heart pounding out of my chest. Bobbing helmets ahead.
The arc of light from that fateful door waxing stubbornly.

Blackness behind eyelids slammed shut. Brief prop blast.
Spinning sky as light returns.
The sight of my feet rising on the horizon.
Then, the pleasing plop of ripstop nylon
    and a canopy of white above.

But, where has all the furious sound gone?
Look there, my lovely aircraft slipping over the horizon.
Seen, but leaving only silence.
But, why is there no sense of motion?
Up here, earth seems fixed forever a thousand feet below.
For the moment I am a resident of the sky,
Drifting along, all alone with my uncommon joy.

PEAK EXPERIENCES, POST MASLOW

The English writer Colin Wilson (1931–2013) could be called a spiritual heir to Maslow, but neither would likely describe their relationship as master and disciple. That would be misleading because Wilson's writings on peak experiences, although he did not use that term, predated Maslow. But Maslow died forty-three years before Wilson, so "heir" seems an appropriate term. They talked on the telephone, met, and collaborated on occasion. Wilson was called on later to write a biography of Maslow.

Characterizing Colin Wilson, who was such a free spirit, is difficult. At age twenty-four he published his first book, and an instant classic: *The Outsider* (1956). Although Wilson was a total unknown, his book was a bestseller, spurred on by rave reviews. Thereafter, for the next fifty-plus years, he tried to repeat that success, eventually drifting into books about the occult and scientology.

Despite the lack of gravitas of some of his later writings, *The Outsider* remains a classic. It was written when existentialism was in its heyday. To put the time in perspective: Camus' *L'Étranger* was published in 1942, Sartre's *La Nausée* was translated into English in 1949, and Becket's *Waiting for Godot* was first performed in 1953. Wilson's unique approach was to illuminate startling peak experiences of both celebrities and well-known fictional characters. These brief positive experiences of the famous stood in stark contrast with their angst over the meaninglessness of life. Here's how Wilson himself later described his classic.

> Now my first book *The Outsider* (1956) was also basically about peak experiences. It was a study of those Romantic poets and painters of the 19th Century who experienced marvelous states of 'transcendent consciousness,' moods in which it was self-evident that the whole universe was a wonderful place, so exciting that it seemed absurd that anyone should ever want to die. Yet when they woke up the next morning, they would find themselves wondering what on earth they meant by it. It now seemed an illusion. Life was now self-evidently trivial and dull and ordinary, and it seemed grimly apparent that we were all trapped in this. This accounted for the despair that led to high levels of suicide and death by tuberculosis among such 'outsiders.'
>
> —Colin Wilson
> *Super Consciousness* (2009, p. 4&5)

Wilson's real-life artists and fictional characters in *The Outsider* experienced what might be called existential angst, although some may have been unaware of such a concept. What they were aware of was a strange distaste for the life that surrounded them and a pervading feeling of meaninglessness. What would carry them to the edge of insanity, though, was a random rapturous event that seemed to contain all they were seeking but would then disappear in a few moments.

Some outsiders were driven in their suffering to produce great innovations or works of art. A partial list from *The Outsider* would include Hermann Hesse, T. E. Lawrence ("Lawrence of Arabia"), Vincent van Gogh, Frederick Nietzsche, Fyodor Dostoyevsky, and W. B. Yeats.

To illustrate an outsider in fiction, Wilson (p. 22–25) examines a character in Jean-Paul Sartre's *La Nausée* named Roquentin, who experiences a strange sensation of nausea about his surroundings. "[The] nausea is not *inside* me, I feel it *out there*, in the wall, in the suspenders, everywhere around me. It makes itself one with the café; I am the one who is within it."

Referring to the café's owner, Roquentin says, "When his place empties, his head empties, too." He believes that the people around him are content to let outside events control and define their lives. As Roquentin's despair deepens in one café scene, someone puts on a record, "Some of These Days," sung by a female Negro vocalist. Roquentin continues, "When the voice was heard in the silence I felt my body harden and the nausea vanish; suddenly it was almost unbearable to be so hard, so brilliant . . . I am *in* the music. Globes of fire turn in the mirrors, encircled by rings of smoke."

[Wilson comments:] Only something as instinctively rhythmic as the blues can give him a sense of order that doesn't seem false. But even that may be a temporary refuge; deeper nervous exhaustion would [eventually] cause the collapse of the sense of order. . . . Yet Roquentin had had his glimpse of meaning and order in "Some of These Days." . . . Roquentin wonders [in his journal]: why shouldn't he create something like that; something rhythmic, purposive—a novel, perhaps, that men could read later and feel: There was an attempt to bring order into chaos? (24–5)

La Nausée ends as Roquentin reflects on the event in his journal. His idea of writing a novel hints at Sartre's doctrine of commitment in a world devoid of meaning. (Perhaps our own personal peak experiences can help guide us in that commitment, as it did for Roquentin.)

However one may feel about Wilson's concept of the outsider, you have to admire the work he did in unearthing some fascinating examples of famous people's peak experiences. We turn now to Frederick Nietzsche (p. 126) and an event he refers to in a letter written to a friend in 1865, age twenty-five or so.

> Yesterday an oppressive storm hung over the sky, and I hurried to a neighboring hill called Leutch. . . . At the top of the hill I found a hut, where a man was killing two [goat] kids while his sons watched him. The storm broke with a tremendous crash, discharging the thunder and hail, and I had an indescribable sense of well-being and zest. . . . Lightening and tempest are different worlds, free powers without morality. Pure will without the confusion of intellect—how happy, how free.

We could speculate that this key peak experience was perhaps the catalyst for Nietzsche's attraction to "pure will," as opposed to Schopenhauer's distaste for the will. The powerful release of amoral forces of nature came to Nietzsche's attention against a background of blood and suffering of the kids and the curious fascination of the boys watching the killing. All glory to our "Will to Power." It can release us from our intellect, "sicklied over with the pale cast of thought," and banish weak-kneed concern about the pain and suffering of others.

Another example (p. 244) of a famous person's peak experience is a poem by W. B. Yeats called "Vacillation" (1950),

My fiftieth birthday had come and gone,
I sat, a solitary man,
In a crowded London shop, An open book and empty cup
On the marble table-top.

While on the shop and street I gazed
My body of a sudden blazed;
And twenty minutes more or less
It seemed so great my happiness, That I was blessed and could bless.

Yeats also wrote: "There is another world, but it is in this one." Finally, Wilson recounts a peak experience of the great Hindu mystic, Ramakrishna. In 1843 at the age of seven, he was walking near a small village in Bengal.

One day in June or July. . . . I was walking along a narrow path separating the patty fields, eating some puffed rice, which I was carrying in a basket. Looking up at the sky, I saw a beautiful sombre thundercloud. As it spread rapidly over the whole sky, a flight of snow-white cranes flew overhead in front of it. It presented such a beautiful contrast [stunned his senses] that my mind wandered to far-off regions. Lost to outward sense, I fell down, and the puffed rice was scattered in all directions. (p.252)

The Outsider was published in 1956. Maslow's *Religion, Values, and Peak-Experiences* was published eight years later. Maslow was not aware of Wilson's work until the latter half of the 1960s. Then they communicated for a number of years until Maslow died in 1970. The contact Wilson had with Maslow and his research on peak experiences influenced his interpretation of an event that occurred to him.

> On New Year's Day, 1979, I was trapped by snow in a remote Devon farm house, near a village called Sheepwash, where I had gone to lecture to extra-mural students . . . I returned to the farm house for lunch before setting out [for home] in the darkening afternoon. The snow on the narrow country lane had been churned up by traffic, but was still treacherous. In places where it was still untouched, it was hard to see where the road ended and the ditch began. So I was forced to drive with total obsessive attention. . . . Finally back to the main Exeter road, where I was able to relax, I noticed everything I looked at seemed curiously real and interesting. *The two hours of concentrated attention had somehow 'fixed' my consciousness in a higher state of awareness.* There was also an immense feeling of optimism, a conviction that most human problems are due to vagueness, slackness, inattention . . . Even now, merely thinking about the experience is enough to bring back the insight and renew the certainty. [Emphasis mine.]
> —Colin Wilson
> *Super Consciousness* (2009, pp. 180–1)

Wilson was suggesting that under the right circumstances, sustained concentration of attention, like the two hours in his Sheepwash experience, could temporarily freeze your consciousness in an altered state for some time thereafter. He apparently saw this as a conscious way to induce a peak-like experience. This is not what I think of as a peak experience, but rather something more like a runner's high. Nevertheless, his suggestion does have interesting implications that we will return to later.

A video of Colin Wilson giving a lecture in 1994 on existentialism and peak experiences can be found on *You Tube* (http://www. youtube.com/

watch?v=btNpJ0iUaRQ). In the lecture, he provided a fascinating account of a meeting he'd had thirty-six years earlier with Albert Camus, the French existentialist. They were discussing *L'Étranger* (The Stranger/Outsider). When the main character's (Meursault) mother dies, he is totally unaffected, as he is by most everything in his life. When Meursault asks his supervisor for time off for the funeral, for example, he apologizes unnecessarily because he doesn't understand the importance others give to a parent's death. His memorable description as to the timing of her death was: "Mother died today. Or maybe it was yesterday. I can't be sure."

Meursault also doesn't know how to respond to his girlfriend's question of whether or not he loves her. He relates the experience thusly: "Then she asked me again if I loved her; I replied much as before, that her question meant nothing to me, or next to nothing, but I suppose I didn't."

The novel winds down to a tragic end when he goes on trial for a murder that is really more a case of self-defense. Meursault is found guilty, partially because his indifference to the man's death makes him seem a cold, callous killer. His callousness to his mother's death is entered as further evidence of his disregard for human life. The night before he is scheduled to be executed, Meursault has what could be called a peak experience. Earlier in the day he had uncharacteristically lost his temper when a cocksure priest called on him to repent for his crimes. What crimes? He knew he had done nothing wrong, certainly not enough to deserve execution, and that triggered his rage. The rage, though, released something inside, and at night as he looked up at the stars, he found peace.

> It was as if the great rush of anger had washed me clean, emptied me of hope, and gazing up at the dark sky. . . . I laid my heart open to the benign indifference of the universe. To feel it so like myself . . . made me realize I had been happy, that I was happy still.

Wilson asked Camus how he could maintain that life was meaningless when various characters in *L'Etranger* had about six peak experiences in which they were overwhelmed by episodes of poignant meaning? In reply, Camus pointed out the window of his Paris apartment to a pathetic man hunched over on the sidewalk. To Wilson he looked like a "Teddy Boy," an English subculture in the 1950s known for their exaggerated pegged trousers and very long coats. Camus explained that what worked for that poor soul must also work for him, and vice versa. Wilson became incensed at this reply and said, and I paraphrase: "You mean to tell me that if Einstein couldn't explain his Theory of Relativity to a Parisian Teddy Boy, he should chuck it?"

TRANSCENDENCE

So, we have found transcendence at last; it was with us all along in the form of our peak experiences. Wait, you say, you don't have to reach self-actualization or have a degree in philosophy to know about peak experiences. Not unless you never understood their importance in the centuries-old metaphysical debate about the existence of transcendence.

There is a letdown. These peak experiences last for only a few moments, perhaps a couple of minutes in a lifetime for most. Some might like to settle down permanently in transcendence-land. True, it might seem nice to enter that state permanently, but, believe it or not, you might not really want to. Probably the best descriptive term for this permanent state is nirvana.

Schopenhauer surmised that if you could put yourself in a permanently will-less state, you could enter a nirvana. But even he, if given the chance, probably would not have been willing to give up the pleasures of the good life and his peccadilloes for life in such an unknown state. One who reportedly was known to have achieved the power to enter nirvana was Siddhartha Gautama, the Buddha. Even he stepped back. Like the hero of Plato's Cave, he rushed back to help his fellow man, rather than losing himself in the brilliant light of nirvana. The Buddha was more successful with his compatriots than Plato's hero, as the story goes, since enough people listened to found a major religion.

But how do ideas about transcendence help people when they wake up Monday morning, running late, needing to get the children off to school, fighting the commuter traffic into work, and don't undergo another peak experience for another decade or two?

CHAPTER NINE

BACK TO REAL LIFE

ON THE PATH TO TRANSCENDENCE

Progressing toward a practical approach to transcendence, we've moved through the philosophy of Kant-Schopenhauer and through the psychology of Maslow-Wilson. Philosophy teaches us that despite the skepticism of postmodern academics, the existence of transcendence cannot be disproved, and Kant suggested its existence is implied by what we know of the phenomenal world. On the other hand, it cannot be proved or accessed by rational means, either. Alongside this conundrum is the undeniable and eternal longing, deep in the human psyche, for some form of transcendence. In everyday, non-spiritual life, this longing can manifest itself in a fascination with the lives of the rich and famous, as if through a study of their activities and imitation of their dress or lifestyles, some of their "super humanity" can be infused into our lives. Other, more-spiritual, paths include church membership and meditation. By now, most people no longer try to explain these spiritual paths as scientifically rational. Instead they are called "faith-based endeavors."

The main take-away from the psychology we covered earlier is that some believe peak experiences contain intimations of transcendence. From a practical point of view, however, the usefulness of peak experiences is limited by their short duration and random occurrence. That is not to say their profound blessing is totally lost. The notion of a lasting benefit is conveyed in the following poem by Eunice Tietjens. Her ascent of Mount Tai Shan in China was a peak experience, and once "having known" transcendence, her everyday life was forever changed.

THE MOST-SACRED MOUNTAIN[62]

SPACE, and the twelve clean winds of heaven,
And this sharp exultation, like a cry, after the slow six thousand steps of
   climbing!
This is Tai Shan, the beautiful, the most holy.

Below my feet the foothills nestle, brown with flecks of green;
And lower down the flat brown plane, the floor of earth, stretches away
   to blue infinity.
Beside me in this airy space the temple roofs cut their slow curves against
   the sky,
And one black bird circles above the void.

Space, and the twelve clean winds are here;
And with them broods eternity—a swift, white peace, a presence manifest.
The rhythm ceases here. Time has no place. This is the end that has no end.
Here, when Confucius came, a half thousand years before the Nazarene,

---

62   *The Second Book of Modern Poetry*, 1922, ed. by Jessie B. Rittenhouse. The "twelve clean winds of heaven" refer to the twelve points of the ancient compass. "Tai Shan" is a mountain in China near Qufu, Confucius's home.

He stepped, with me, thus into timelessness.

The stone beside us waxes old, the carven stone says:

"On this spot once Confucius stood and felt the smallness of the world
below."

The stone grows old: Eternity is not for stones.

But I shall go down from this airy place, this swift white peace, this
stinging exultation.

And time will close about me, and my soul stir to the rhythm of the daily
round.

Yet, *having known*, life will not press so close, And always I shall feel time
ravel thin around me;

For once I stood in the white windy presence of eternity.

Peak experiences can lead to total life make-overs, as occurred for Fyodor
Dostoyevsky, following a close encounter with a firing squad, and for Blaise
Pascal, after a miraculous cure of his illness. But most people don't recognize
the possible elements of transcendence in their peak experiences.

Those who do may be inspired to try to make transcendent experiences
a meaningful part of their everyday lives, often by trying to repeat them
somehow. Like the philosophers of the past, they will soon find this approach
unrewarding. Others may turn to spirituality with a more dedicated practice
of religion or meditation or contemplation, to move closer to transcendence,
once they've given up trying to reason their way there. It is too easy, though,
to quickly lose yourself in the details of practice while forgetting what brought
you there to begin with. *What exactly are we seeking?* To answer this question,
let's go back to the time when these notions of transcendence took a form
that's essentially unchanged today: the Axial Age.

THE AXIAL AGE

The idea of an Axial Age is fairly recent and is attributed to Karl Jaspers (1881–1969), a German psychiatrist and philosopher. "Axial" can be paraphrased as "pivotal." His use of the term first appeared in a German publication in 1949, which was translated into English in 1953 under the title, *The Origin and Goal of History*.

Jaspers' book focused attention on the major turning point in human consciousness, when our ideas of transcendence were first articulated and, for the most part, finalized. He dated these developments to the period between 800 and 200 BCE. What he and others found so profound was that these concepts of transcendence took form in four separate locations spread across the known world, *independently and simultaneously*.[63]

Specifically, he was referring first to the ancient Greek philosophy we have already touched on. Then, moving east from there to Judaic monotheism in Asia Minor, to the Hindu Upanishads and Buddhism in India, and finally to Confucianism and Taoism in China. These concepts have been repeatedly embellished over the centuries and appear today as bewilderingly varied and complex. But in the beginning, they shared a simple core message that can still speak to

---

63   There is a recorded encounter between two of the spiritual centers of the Axial Age. It took place circa 327 BCE after Greeks, led by Alexander the Great, arrived at the Indian capital city of Taxila. These Greeks were particularly well-trained in philosophy. Alexander's tutor was none other than Aristotle. And his emissary, Onesicitus, had studied under Diogenes. They had heard intriguing rumors of marvelous new developments in transcendence taking place in Hindu India. Onesicitus was sent by Alexander to seek out leaders of this movement and to start a comparative-philosophy dialogue. Things probably didn't work out the way Alexander imagined. Onesicitus was led by city officials to an outcropping of rock on the outskirts of Taxila. The Hindu leaders were seated stark-naked on sunbaked rock so hot that the Greeks could not have walked on it without their boots. Through an interpreter, Onesicitus started the dialogue by reviewing some of the insights of Greek philosophy. As fellow philosophers, the Indian ascetics marveled at the acuity of the Greeks. But, they were very perplexed by one inconsistency: Why would Pythagoras, Socrates, and Plato—who were obviously at the forefront of philosophical thought—deny themselves ultimate sublimity by remaining clothed? (This account was attributed to Strabo, who traveled with Alexander on his campaigns, by Joseph Campbell in *The Masks of God: Oriental Mythology*, 1962, p. 277.)

us today as it did to others 2,500 years ago. For a beginning summary, I like the description of the axial model by Professor Stephen Erikson of Pomona College:

> We start with an ancient model, which was developed somewhere between 800—200 BCE. In the axial model, a sharp distinction was made between this world and a world beyond, and the idea arose that, although we are in this world, we are not altogether of this world. According to this model, human life is a journey that leads from appearance to reality, bondage to liberation, confusion to insight, and from darkness to light.
>
> Though we are in, we are not altogether of this world, even if, in no literal sense, any other world exists. This statement captures what I will be referring to as the axial sensibility: the sense that we find ourselves caught up largely in appearances and are trapped in and subject to various forms of bondage, such as political, psychological, and possibly spiritual ones. Coupled with this sense is the further sense that there must be an elsewhere or another and better way of being in this world as it is now, one that better engages reality and gives us a sense of liberation rather than confinement. This axial sense may prove to be but an inchoate and unrealistic longing, but it has and continues to be experienced by many as genuine and inescapable. It has often been described as a longing for a belonging, driven in part by a sense of not belonging to the world as it is, of being displaced by it.
>
> —*Philosophy as a Guide to Living*
> The Teaching Company (2006, pp 1&5)

The importance of this axial model, and the movements based on it, cannot be overstated. It was the spiritual mindset of much of the world until modern times. Christianity was rooted in Axial Age Judaism, and the Roman Catholic Church later also incorporated parts of Greek Platonism into its orthodoxy. In Western Europe, Christianity became universally accepted after Emperor

Constantine legalized it in 313 CE and was converted himself before his death. Some have even suggested that Western Europe was essentially a theocracy in the Middle Ages under the Roman Catholic Church until the time of the Reformation and the Enlightenment.

The history of organized Christianity in the modern era, though, has been that of a slow decline in influence. It has changed from an authoritarian, spiritual model to a much more liberal and do-good social model, at least in the mainline Protestant denominations of the West. Churches still benefit, however, from our reverence for an ancient institution that has survived, even in significantly changed form, for almost 2,000 years. Of course, farther east, it can be a different story. Islam, like Christianity and Judaism, traces its roots back to Abraham but has experienced much less secularization. For example, in Islamic countries, the nonreligious are subject to government-sanctioned discrimination. Reuters (December 9, 2013) reported that a recent survey found that in 13 Islamic countries, a professed atheist, called an apostate, can be executed.

The original axial model, though, was and is a different animal from the institutional religious trappings and reinterpretations that followed. For me, personally, the "longing for a belonging" in the axial model speaks directly to me, quite apart from any religious feelings. From an early age, I was haunted by the notion that I was born at the wrong time. There is little point detailing these childhood fantasies, but the practical upshot was that I believed I had been given the wrong skill set for the time and place I found myself. For example, in-your-face posturing seemed to be highly prized, while I tended to be introverted. What seemed to be expected of me socially and in my future life work appeared ill-mannered and banal, like the Babbitt character in Sinclair Lewis's satire of the modern American businessman. On the other hand, my favorite radio character was the Lone Ranger, the penultimate strong, silent type.

The cost of my maladjustment was more than just feeling out of place; it was downright painful. The outward manifestations of my personality, withdrawal, social awkwardness, and phlegmatic demeanor, fostered ridicule

Reprinted with permission of Chris Madden at chris@chrismadden.co.uk

in my prep school years and lost promotions in my corporate career years. In later life, I was able to project a veneer of success in society's terms, especially after starting my own firm. But the feeling of not belonging was always there. In reality I did belong in the usual sense, but I just couldn't feel it inside. My father's position in the community, along with my Wharton MBA, would have assured acceptance in my hometown, but I chose to move 700 miles away. I was somehow convinced there were watchful eyes in my hometown just waiting for me to fail, and I could vividly imagine the excruciating shame

I would feel if I did. It would simply be unbearable. So, I chose to move far away, where I could succeed or fail, and people wouldn't care if I failed.

From the pain of ridicule in prep school and of the feeling of being taken advantage of in corporate life, I experienced injury, not to my body, but to my soul. I felt at the mercy of others and believed I lacked the social skills to influence them favorably.[64] To me the real world appeared, using Schopenhauer's phrase, as "something that should not have been." Simultaneously, the hope arose in me that if I could create conditions in which I was not so financially dependent on the real or imagined opinions of others, such as my bosses, I could find happiness. Not only find happiness, but I could begin restorative treatment of the wounds to my soul. This was the motivating force behind my desire for early retirement and a search for transcendence. This leisure I aspired to would become my "elsewhere."

TO LEAVE THIS WORLD PHYSICALLY

In the axial model, a sharp distinction was made between this world and a world beyond.

—Erikson (p. 1)

---

[64]   Over the years I tried to improve myself to meet society's social norms. My bible was *How to Win Friends and Influence People* by Dale Carnegie (1936), probably reading it a dozen times. I also attended their twelve-week Leadership Training Course, winning Best Speaker of the course among the forty-two participants. I also spent several years in Toastmasters, even serving as President of the local club. I cherish these experiences; but as far as making me more extroverted in everyday social situations, it was a bust.
Recently, after reading Susan Cain's *Quiet* (2012), I have come to realize that my past problems, described above, are a classical description of a well-researched personality "disorder" called introversion. My problematic skillset turns out to be quite common. It is an inborn personality type that I share with up to one-quarter of the population. Unfortunately, most of us are unaware that so many others are also born this way and assume we are personally negligent for not being more extroverted. Compounding this ignorance is the fact that America is considered the most extroverted country on earth outside of Australia. Here, the extroverted ideal rules. But, accepting my introversion— now that I no longer have to hide it—has helped to heal my soul.

The motion picture *Gattaca* (1997) actually addresses in modern terms the notion of travel from "this world" to a "world beyond." The goal in life of the hero, Vincent, played by Ethan Hawke, is to reach the world beyond in space by physically leaving this world. To do so, he must first become an astronaut. But, in this future, society was obsessed with genetic engineering. The genetic requirements for astronauts are extremely high, and Vincent is barely average in this regard. "They have discrimination down to a science," he said, referring to the genoism in his society. He is forced in the beginning to take low-skill janitorial jobs. The story revolves around his struggles to deceive the genetically elite with purchased genetic samples, become an astronaut, and finally blast off into space. For me, the story is an allegory[65] for *spiritual* travel to a world beyond while overcoming the gravitational pull of this world. Vincent sees it as a trip home from a world that has no place in it for him. "Of course they say every atom in our body was once part of a [supernova] star. Maybe I'm not leaving . . . maybe I'm going home."

During one college summer I experimented with physically leaving my world. My parents saw me off at the train station believing I was going to Charlotte, North Carolina, to meet up with a fraternity brother to then drive out west, as I had done the previous summer with two other friends. I checked most of my luggage into a train station locker after I reached Charlotte, kept a duffle bag of clothes, and, alone, stuck out my thumb for rides heading west. With $75 in cash (about $600 in 2016 dollars), but no credit card and no job prospects, my goal was to head west and return with more than $75. I didn't escape earth's gravity like Vincent in *Gattaca*, but I did my best, even changing my name. Name changing became a problem when I finally landed a construction job in Hutchinson, Kansas, with a crew from Minnesota erecting grain storage buildings. My boss needed my real name and number for Social Security reporting purposes. Whether or not he believed my story of

---

65   *The Pilgrim's Progress from This World to That Which Is to Come* by John Bunyan (1678) is an example of a Christian travel allegory.

why I went by a different name, my earnings from that year showed up on my Social Security record when I checked years later. By the end of the summer I had lost fifteen pounds from hard labor and economizing on food costs, but I was able to return with $150, even after paying bus fare home. The $150 went to buying a green three-piece business suit, which, I guess, symbolized a return to my fate. To find a different route to a world beyond, I would have to wait until retirement.

BUDDHA (563–493 BCE)

We have already discussed some of the contributions of ancient Greek philosophers to the Axial Age. Of the other contributing philosophies and religions, I believe that Buddhism provides the clearest illustration of the axial model. For example, "elsewhere" can be paraphrased as nirvana. At the epicenter of Buddhism is the enlightenment of Siddhartha Gautama (Buddha). The story in the beginning is not about religion as much as about transcendence. We can start the story at the point Gautama, the future Buddha, experiences a wound to his soul when his enjoyable and safe existence is shattered by abrupt first encounters outside his wealthy father's compound with disease, old age, and death. He decides he must make a complete break with home and family or be forever smothered by their protection and their denial of the suffering around them. He sets out from home to find a cure for the pain in his soul.

From the beginning of his journey, Gautama realized that, despite his intentions, his old desire for pleasure and security traveled with him even after leaving his father's protective domain. These desires were relentless, but satisfying them would mean sublimating the pain in his soul and turning a blind eye to suffering around him. It was his insight that following desire can lead to an endless cycle of pleasure and pain. He first had to extinguish the insistent burning of those desires before he would be able to find enlightenment and peace for his soul.

Others before him had realized that extinguishing the flame of desire was the key to peace. Luckily, Gautama had experts or masters he could seek out to help him on his journey, or so he thought. The most promising spiritual technology of the time was practiced by wandering yogis. Their teachings were based on the Hindu *Upanishads* and the discipline of yoga, both of which were among the Hindu contributions to the Axial Age. He sought out the two yogis Arada and Udraka, most renowned for their spiritual mastery. He quickly learned their methods and progressed beyond these masters to the ultimate stages of trance, where desire and the self were extinguished. Yet, Gautama did not feel he had found what he was seeking. First, he had created these extreme mental states artificially, by personal effort and trained discipline. So, they were self-induced trances and not part of nature. Second, as soon as he left his trances, his petty concerns about bodily pleasures returned. He had achieved an impressive degree of control over his mind, but base desires remained.

Perhaps, he needed to learn control over his body as well. So he sought out the most acclaimed masters of another type of renouncer called ascetics, those who practiced conscious mortification of the flesh to build discipline over bodily desires. Unfortunately for Gautama, he picked a group of radical ascetics, whose techniques included lying on a bed of nails, eating their bodily waste, and fasting to the point of starvation. He followed these techniques to a state of near death, reaching a stage where he could think of nothing at all except the pain in his body. Relying on the best spiritual advice of his day, Gautama had wrecked his health and come to a spiritual dead end.

One could imagine Gautama deciding to call an end to this madness and returning home; after all, he had given it his best effort. But something inside would not allow him to do that. He did decide, however, that he must find his own way forward. There could be no outside help for him. But, what could he do? What happened next was quite remarkable and involves a version of Gautama's story that is not well-known.[66] As Gautama started to regain his health, and while in a state of doubting everything he thought he ever knew, he recalled a long-forgotten childhood memory, a peak experience:

> [H]is nurse had left him under the shade of a rose apple tree while she watched the ceremonial plowing of the fields before the spring planting. The little boy sat up and saw the young shoots of grass had been torn up by the plow, and insects had been killed. Gazing at the carnage, Gotama had felt a strange pang of grief, as though his own relatives had died. The surge of selfless empathy brought him a moment of spiritual release. It was a beautiful day, and the child had felt true joy welling up in him.
>
> —Karen Armstrong
> *The Great Transformation* (2006, p. 329)

The recollection of this childhood episode was pivotal for Gautama. He realized that he had *already* experienced, in a crude and temporary form, what he had been seeking all those years after leaving home to become a renouncer. For a few moments in his childhood, the flame of desire had been extinguished, as a deep empathy for the suffering of other creatures, grass and insects, had overwhelmed his senses. Could this possibly be the way to enlightenment? he asked himself.

The Greek philosophers believed that our most important new insights are really only a recalling of what we already knew in our soul. Unlike the traditional accounts, this was not a matter of sitting under the bodhi tree and achieving

---

66　This version of Gautama's enlightenment by Karen Armstrong dovetailed so nicely with my belief in the importance of peak experiences that I wondered about her sources. As well as I can determine, her account was based on the *Majjhima Nikaya*, a Sanskrit scripture (circa 50 BCE.), Discourse 36. (Earlier Discourse 26 contains a different account, more in line with the traditional story of sudden enlightenment under the Bodhi tree.) Ms. Armstrong also referenced Joseph Campbell's version in *The Mask of God: Oriental Mythology*, 1962, p. 277, whose source was the Indian author, Ashroghosha, circa 100 CE.

nirvana overnight. Rather, it was finding a new direction, and compassion was the central characteristic of this new direction. "He should foster helpful (*Kusala*) states of mind such as the disinterested impulse of compassion that had surfaced so naturally, and at the same time avoid any mental or physical states that would impede this liberation," as Karen Armstrong describes it (p. 331). In other words, he should avoid exotic trances and radical asceticism that could interfere with more fruitful compassionate contemplation. Like the Greeks, he settled on a middle path.

The religions and philosophy of the Axial Age taught moderation in appetite and a disciplined control of one's more primitive impulses. To reach nirvana, Gautama believed one must go further. People's baser nature has its own built-in cheering section, like perpetual barkers in a carnival. We must try to offset this advantage by consciously focusing on the polar opposites of these negative instincts. For example, lying to others to gain advantage is a negative impulse. But people should go further than only not lying; we should also strive for helpful discourse out of respect for others. Of course, the parents of our actions are our thoughts. We should aim for mindfulness, an awareness of our hateful, envious impulses, and put down thoughts about others, and about ourselves. Using Schopenhauer's words, one should be aware of "the will" that operates at the border of one's consciousness.

The idea is not to block these desires, which may only strengthen them, but to be aware of them and to move on. And, as the boy Gautama under the rose apple tree discovered, moving on to compassionate thoughts can act like antimatter in the presence of base desire, and for a while peace can be achieved.

Reportedly, even with this more effective direction, Gautama did not achieve the supreme enlightenment he was seeking for another seven years. This was no born-again experience. The last piece to the puzzle was extinguishing belief in the self. I doubt that I could ever achieve this level of detachment, but I think I can follow the logic that if you extinguished belief in a self, nothing would ever bother you again.

In the end, the story of Gautama's life is about searching for an elsewhere and finding it. This is full transcendence.

> For many of his contemporaries, the Buddha was a haven of peace in a violent, sorrowful world. The search for a place apart, separate from the world, and yet wondrously within it, that is impartial, utterly fair, calm, and that fills us with a confidence that, against all odds, there is value in our lives, was what many people in the Axial Age sought when they looked for God, Brahman, or nibbana [liberation].
>
> —Armstrong (p. 342)

MAKING IT ALL WORK

> *I grew in those seasons like corn in the night.*
>
> —Henry David Thoreau
> *Walden* (1854, p.120)

To write this book, and to read this book, demonstrates a hope for something hard to find from the usual sources of friends, acquaintances, and media. That something is meaningful spirituality. From the usual sources, the answer is easy: Join a religion and attend regularly. Somehow that answer doesn't work for me and, I suspect, for many others. For me it's not *meaningful* spirituality, that is, more important than, say, my material security.

Philosophy has been the source of meaningful spirituality in the past. Others have made it work for them. What comes to mind are the Transcendentalists' response to Kant and the early Communists' response to Marx. Also, Thoreau's *Essay on Civil Disobedience* (1849) provided a philosophical framework to help guide Mahatma Gandhi and Martin Luther King, Jr. in their leadership of peaceful mass movements in India and for blacks in America. But that kind of spirituality is missing in current American society. In this regard, the current

"You're kidding... I've got a masters in philosophy too!"

Reprinted with permission of CartoonStock Ltd at cartoonstock.com

crop of professional philosophers is so non-spiritual as to be a joke. According to a recent survey by PhilPapers,[67] 90 percent of American professors of philosophy identify themselves as belonging to the analytic school. That is, they address issues of language, linguistics, and natural science, rather than issues of life's meaning. For example, their choice for favorite dead philosopher was not Aristotle (2nd), Plato (13th), or even Kant (3rd), but David Hume, a 17th-century Scottish philosopher and economist with a decidedly skeptical view of anything

67   See PhilPapers website (www.philpapers.org) for November 2009 survey.

not empirically provable. He was a forerunner of English analytic philosophy, which dominates English-speaking countries today. Contemporary American philosophers have little use for idealistic philosophies, including existentialism. They also have no use for religion, with three-quarters identifying themselves as actual or probable atheists. That's evangelical compared to the National Academy of Sciences where only 7 percent of members believe in God.[68]

Most analytic philosophers, apparently, would deny the existence of transcendence and would argue that efforts to find it were meaningless. Yet, the most renowned member of that school, Ludwig Wittgenstein, did not fit this characterization.

LUDWIG WITTGENSTEIN (1889–1951)

Three Cambridge professors, Bertrand Russell, G.E. Moore, and Ludwig Wittgenstein, are credited with founding the English analytic school of philosophy in the early 20th century. This is the modern version of the skeptical enlightenment philosophy of the late 18th century that included David Hume, among others. This school is so dominant today that a philosophy professor on an American campus who expressed belief in religion or idealism would probably risk his or her professional reputation. But Wittgenstein, regarded by some as the greatest of this school, was a natural maverick and unconcerned about his reputation. He was very religious and exceedingly ethical. He became deeply committed to Christianity as an adult after reading Tolstoy. Although he was one of the foremost geniuses of his day, his ethics led him

---

68   Anthony Gottlieb, *Intelligent Life* magazine, Spring 2010. According to some surveys, 80 percent of Americans believe in God. "However, despite this seemingly high level of religiosity, only 9 percent of Americans in a 2008 poll said religion was the most important thing in their life, compared with 45 percent who said family was paramount in their life and 17 percent who said money and their career was paramount." (*Wikipedia*: "Religion in the United States"). About 43 percent said they attended a church or synagogue in the past week (Gallup) compared to 15 percent in France and 10 percent in the U.K. There may be a high social value in the U.S. for claiming religiosity that accounts for these inconsistencies.

to enlist on the losing (Austrian) side as a private, instead of as an officer, in World War I, and he was awarded several medals for valor. His ethics made him uncomfortable with his enormous inherited wealth, which he gave to his sisters and to charities. Simple living appealed to him; he spent many years living in remote areas of Sweden and Austria and working as a gardener or secondary school teacher. Later in life, he returned to Cambridge, when G.E. Moore retired and a chair in philosophy became available. During World War II, he served the winning (British) side as a lowly hospital orderly.

Wittgenstein did not fit the mold of the typical analytic philosopher today, as evidenced by his letter to a potential publisher of his masterpiece, *Tractatus Logico-Philosophicus* (1921). The letter included this curious summary:

> My work consists of two parts, the one presented here plus all that I have not written. And it is precisely this second part that is the important one.

I believe the second part concerned his mystical side that believed in God and ethics. Transcendence is not a place analytic philosophy could go, and he believed this was the more important part of his work. He went on in *Tractatus* (p. 71) to say: "It is clear ethics cannot be put into words. Ethics is transcendental."

Wittgenstein's most famous quote from *Tractatus* (p. 73) is: "What a man cannot speak about, he must pass over in silence." One cannot speak about transcendence in words. So, what are philosophers supposed to make of signs of transcendence, such as peak experiences? The answer is to accept that these experiences can come on their own without the need for language.

> There are, indeed, things that cannot be put into words. They make themselves manifest. They are what is mystical.
>
> —Wittgenstein (73)

To find published help today in our postmodern world with the big issues of life, outside organized religion, one would need to drop down in gravitas to the feel-good pop gurus like Dr. Phil, Tony Robbins, or Wayne Dyer. But to give them their due, they have successfully adopted their message to meet a real need for quick treatment of self-esteem problems in our fast-paced lives. Their self-improvement approach to personal philosophy and happiness is practical and logical, not spiritual. I would characterize the approaches as variations of Norman Vincent Peale's "positive thinking," where one endeavors to neutralize negative thoughts by thinking offsetting positive ones. This does work, as long as one maintains the conscious willpower to think positive thoughts. Over time, though, willpower flags, but the will never does. Then doubt and discouragement creep in, not unlike what happens on diets. These techniques reflect our society's preference for using rational and extroverted means to address spiritual issues.

The Transcendentalist movement may have represented the last time in America that philosophy was seen as possibly holding significant answers to life's questions. One has to wonder what it was about this group that made them such a force for egalitarianism in the nineteenth century. Let's return to the Transcendentalists and to Thoreau.

HENRY DAVID THOREAU (1817–1862)

People sold on the ultimate authority of reason and sensory input can never experience transcendence, except possibly when hit in the face by a peak experience. Those of us who want to have the faith of the Transcendentalists must build it on our own, with little company. The Transcendentalists built their belief two centuries ago based on agreement with Kant's conclusions that reason could never lead one to an understanding of other realities or of transcendence. But, if not reason, what can lead one to transcendence? These people from Concord, Massachusetts, were trying to experience it with non-rational and non-analytical methods. I believe their spiritual leader down this path was Henry David Thoreau. He was the master of seeking such an experience. Here is how he described passing one morning in his cabin on Walden Pond:

> I sat on my sunny doorway from sunrise to noon, rapt in revery, amidst the pines and hickories and sumachs, while the birds sang around or flitted noiseless through the house until by the sun falling at my west window, or the sound of some traveller's wagon on the distant highway, I was reminded of the lapse of time. *I grew in those seasons like corn in the night*, and they were far better than any of the work of the hands would have been. [Italics mine.]
>
> —Henry David Thoreau
> *Walden* (1854, p.120)

Only when the sun appeared in his west window in the afternoon did Thoreau realize that hours had passed since he first sat down. Few, if any, of us can escape the constant chatter of the will and concern for the time to forget ourselves for that long. Even if Thoreau exaggerated, he gave the world a wonderful description of a meditation ideal.

Thoreau had built his cabin on Walden Pond shortly before moving there on July 4, 1845. He knew that when he committed himself to this wilderness experience, he could mainly pursue either of two goals. One, he could see the experience as a survival challenge, confronting nature with few resources other than his innate skills; not only surviving, but also prevailing like a Robinson Crusoe. The two years could have been spent improving the cabin, clearing more acres than he was obligated to, and planting more crops.

But Thoreau "heard a different drummer" and chose Goal Two. As he put it, he wanted to look at life in its simplest form "and see if I could learn what it had to teach." His method was simple direct observation, as shown above, of what happened to be in and around him, unadulterated by judgment or the need to codify his observations. He knew any progress in such an endeavor would be imperceptible in the short run, hence his use of an incredible simile, "like corn in the night," to describe his growth. He was clear that he thought he had chosen the more fruitful of the two goals in terms of personal growth.

> They [the seasons of growth] were not time subtracted from my
> life, but so much over and above my usual allowance. I realized what
> the Orientals meant by contemplation and the forsaking of works.
>
> —Thoreau (120)

The setting for Thoreau's experience with transcendence was, of course, Walden Pond. It's a familiar theme: the wilderness as a forge for building one's essential beliefs. In the Bible, Jesus enters the wilderness "for forty days and forty nights" to be tempted by the devil and to prepare himself for the trials to come. Hindu renouncers retired to the forests of India to seek enlightenment. The wilderness holds a fascination for many, and that includes my father and myself. The peak experiences described at the beginning of this book illustrate this fascination. A couple of other peak experiences detailed earlier involved mountain climbing, which I think can also be included in the wilderness-inspired category.

I no longer believe that an extended stay in a true wilderness is a necessity, although it surely can help in forging one's core beliefs. For that matter, Walden Pond was not truly a wilderness. It was within walking distance of Concord. There were many visits to his cabin by friends, and Thoreau would sometimes walk to Ralph Waldo Emerson's home for dinner and conversation. It did, though, provide what Thoreau needed as a refuge from the constant distractions of modern life in order "to front only the essential facts of life."

Others have built their core beliefs during times of forced isolation. Spinoza lived alone in Spartan surroundings in a second-floor flat, eking out a living by grinding lenses. This environment probably served him as well as any wilderness to muffle the constant chatter of a materialistic society. Over the years of lonely research, he developed a deep knowledge of his lifework, a geometric approach to understanding essence. I can imagine him experiencing moments of sublimity as his research progressed to its highest levels.

> After experience had taught me that all things which frequently take place in ordinary life are vain and futile. . . . I determined at last to inquire whether there was anything which might be truly good, and able to communicate its goodness, and by which the mind might be affected to the exclusion of all other things; I determined, I say, to inquire whether I might discover and attain the faculty of enjoying throughout eternity continual supreme happiness.
>
> —Benedictus de Spinoza
> *The Improvement of the Intellect*
> (Circa 1660, p. 1)

Now we come to our own quest. Probably the only encounters we have had with transcendence in our lives have been peak experiences. We could seek to encourage these experiences by sojourns into the wilderness: mountain climbing, safaris in Tanzania or skydiving. Because of the extreme change in venue, the odds of a peak experience are probably improved, but it's still a hit-or-miss proposition. By my wild guess, perhaps one in a hundred mountain climbers ever have a peak experience while mountain climbing. Besides, you can't build a personal philosophy this way. Peak experiences do serve a vital purpose, however, in alerting us to the possibilities of transcendence. They are like billboards on the highway of life. As we speed along, lost in our careers and concerns, they flash out their message to us:

This is not all there is.

I believe that to build a better spiritual life long-term we need, like Thoreau, "to front only the essential facts of life" through meditation and contemplation. This process is not easy; it's opaque, and so slow as to be virtually imperceptible. And how do you ever measure spiritual growth? It's something one just knows. Measurement falls in the rational world, not the spiritual.

MEDITATION

You do need to begin somewhere, though, with a structure. My favored method of contemplation and meditation is the Zen Buddhist form called *zazen*. This method is simple and eminently non-rational. You sit still, probably close your eyes, and pay attention to your breath as you inhale and exhale. You also remain attentive to the present moment and your surroundings (including sounds and bodily sensations). A time period of thirty minutes is as good as any. It helps, particularly in the beginning, to meditate with a group. Westerners need the comfort of having other meditators around them doing the same thing. It's reassuring to know others apparently believe that this type of activity is OK, and not as idiotic as it feels.

In the beginning, *zazen* certainly seems simple: just follow your breath for half an hour. The main initial problems are boredom, sleepiness, and the pain of extended sitting on the floor. With practice over time, the physical problems ease. Then you make the shocking discovery that, even though you may have managed to sit still for thirty minutes, you have completely forgotten to follow your breath. This often occurs within the first minute. Instead, gratuitous thoughts that previously passed unnoticed have highjacked any attention to your breath. You have mentally been somewhere else for most of the thirty minutes.

These random thoughts originate in the will, a la Schopenhauer, with its perpetual message machine bombarding you with plans for tomorrow, painful memories of embarrassing moments, and judgments about the people around you. Attempts to silence this unwanted self-talk will only make things worse by engaging emotions of frustration. It's hopeless to try to silence the will, which is instinctual and not under conscious control. "There is a Talmudic saying: No one is the owner of his instincts."[69]

> People who do it [zazen] quickly realize that much of what goes on in their heads involves random thoughts that often have very little substance. The goal is not so much to 'empty' your head, but to not get caught up in random thoughts that pop into consciousness.
>
> —Sara Lazar, Harvard Medical School
> "Meditation Found to Increase Brain Size"
> *Harvard Gazette*, February 2006.

Practitioners of *zazen* can become so lost in their random ruminations of the will that their meditation is no more helpful than a thirty-minute nap. Many leave practice at this point, especially those who have been sold on the possibility of instantaneous enlightenment. I had dry periods but stuck with it. Eventually, the frustration with the unwanted and random thoughts receded, and I was able to return to following my breath and my present-moment surroundings more quickly.

Then, I began to experiment with ways to enhance my practice. What works for me, although not necessarily for others, is to practice first thing in the morning before my random thought machine has fully cranked up. I immediately follow that with a trip to the YMCA, where I jump on a treadmill and continue my meditation, eyes closed and following my more rapid breath. The doubling up of meditation and exercise usually produces for me a runner's high effect that almost guarantees a great start for the day. Another

---

69 This is a quote from Elie Wiesel (Holocaust survivor and Nobel Peace Prize winner) in a *New York Times* article (May 21, 2011). He was trying to answer a reporter's question as to why political celebrities sometimes take ridiculous risks in their sexual escapades.

technique I find useful is to simply raise my finger when a gratuitous thought interrupts my concentration. It acknowledges the thought without judgment and reminds me to return to following my breath.

There are other benefits. The meditation/workout routine described above produces a psychological benefit for me that goes beyond only a good exercise experience but also lines up the rest of my day. Although I liken it to a runner's high, it's more. Earlier I quoted Colin Wilson's description of his "Sheepwash" experience where after being forced to drive with total concentration for two hours along roads made treacherous by snow: "The two hours of concentrated attention had somehow 'fixed' my consciousness in a higher state of aware-ness." My treadmill is set to automatically wind down after sixty minutes, so I can minimize all distractions, including what time it is. With my eyes closed and my ears plugged, I can experiment with total concentration on my breath and internal sensations. With sufficient concentration, I have found that the psychological payoff that follows this exercise is repeatable every day and lasts for hours, during which I feel centered and at peace. It's not transcendence, but maybe a reflection of it.

Let's say *zazen* practice continues for some time, and you grow spiritually, perhaps similar to the growth Thoreau felt at Walden Pond. To what end? My answer is pure speculation since measurement of progress is impossible. You simply become, I speculate, more of your own person. Think about it. You are relentlessly bombarded by messages generated by others, most of whom are motivated by their own agendas. These messages come at you from acquaintances, opinion makers on electronic media, and advertisers. Plus the internal will is cranking out directives constantly. In my opinion, 90 percent of those messages have a shelf life of less than half a day, most much less than that. We waste our day away processing this endless foreign verbiage and can't find a half-hour to meditate on our unique place in all this. We are not unlike the shadow watchers in Plato's Cave, blanketed by messages 24/7, including dreams. Thoreau reminds us that if you are acquainted with the principles behind the news, murder, politics, and so forth, you learn little more by reading about the various new examples: "To philosophers all *news*, as it is called, is *gossip*." (100).

From our memories, we form a personal concept of our identity, which is really an amalgamation of pieces of external input from the past. We are what the existentialists would call inauthentic, because our responses only reflect back what we are fed from the outside. But, the truth is that we are more than this. With a play on words, my Zen instructor put it this way, "We are more than we think." Only when the constant background chatter is suspended for a moment can we begin to sense a personal identity beyond the mental construct that we believe is us. We can become more authentic, and then we finally have a unique foundation on which to build a personal philosophy.[70]

OTHER BENEFITS OF MEDITATION

Another benefit of *zazen* is that the practice of paying strict attention for thirty minutes may cause you, after a while, to be more attentive for the remaining twenty-three and a half hours of the day. Let's see some of the research that expands on this idea.

I suggested earlier that *zazen* progress was not something that could be measured. But, that doesn't mean it hasn't been tried. Instead of going into a

---

70 Martin Heidegger, a German existentialist discussed later in the Appendix, believed that Cartesian philosophy in the West, with its separation of mind and matter, had caused us to lose touch with our innate wisdom of being in the world, rather than separate from it, an awareness possessed by primitive man. To remember this wisdom, for enlightenment, we must listen to our being without Cartesian preconceptions. "All our heart's courage is the echoing response to the first call of Being which gathers our thinking into the play of the world." (*Poetry, Language, Thought*, 1971 translation by Albert Hofstadter.) Heidegger was fascinated with Eastern philosophy, especially the teachings of Lao Tzu. Whether he had exposure to Zen Buddhism, or would see *zazen* as a method of listening to our being, is unknown to me. ["Cartesian" refers to René Descartes, who articulated the separtion of mind and matter.]

tedious reporting of the results here, please read the "Research on Meditation" topic in *Wikipedia* on the Internet. The bad news is that results of studies attempting to prove health care benefits of meditation in a mind-body relationship have been mixed. "Firm conclusions on the effects of meditation practices in health care cannot be drawn based on the available evidence." These studies were measuring the effect on hypertension, cardiovascular disease, and substance abuse from a variety of meditation methodologies.

The good news is that when the research was more focused, first on mindfulness meditation, like *zazen*, and second on the physical effects in the brain, the results were much more promising. Using brain scan analysis, researchers at Yale and Harvard universities, and Massachusetts General Hospital were able to document "increased thickness of grey matter in parts of the brain that are responsible for attention and processing sensory input. The increase in thickness ranged between .004 and .008 inches . . . [in] individuals with intensive Buddhist 'insight meditation' training." It would be silly to conclude that these new brain cells are empirical proof of growth in the spiritual sense implied by Thoreau. It is intriguing, though, to speculate as to exactly what these new cells are up to.

Perhaps much of the benefit of meditation comes from the simple act of paying attention. Some of the research on improving the brain was reviewed by Sharon Begley in an article for *Newsweek* (January 10 and 17, 2011) entitled "Can You Build a Better Brain?" According to Ms. Begley, there have been many studies on various ways of improving our brains, but most were useless or inconclusive. One of the problems with brain training, found in a government-sponsored study called "Active," was that training your brain to improve one mental skill didn't necessarily transfer to other mental skills. For example, doing crossword puzzles has for ages been recommended for improving mental acuity. But, research demonstrated that doing crossword puzzles improves only your skill at doing crossword puzzles. But the research on paying attention was more promising.

One of the strongest findings in neuroplasticity, the science of how the brain changes its structure and function in response to input, is that attention is almost magical in its ability to physically alter the brain and enlarge functional circuits.

In a classic experiment, scientists found that when monkeys repeatedly practiced fine-tactile perception, the relevant brain region expanded, just as it does when people learn Braille or the violin. Similarly, a region of the auditory cortex expands when we hear a particular tone over and over. . . . But when monkeys simultaneously touched something and listened to tones, only the brain region they were trained on expanded. In other words, identical input—tactile sensations and sounds—produced a different result, expanding a brain area or not, depending on whether attention is being paid.

Ms. Begley's article concluded by highlighting three techniques for building a better brain:

The holy grail of brain training is something that does transfer [to other mental skills], and here there are three good candidates: [First] Simple aerobic exercise, such as walking 45 minutes a day three times a week, improves episodic memory and executive control functions by about 20 percent, finds Art Krammer of the University of Illinois at Urbana-Champaign.

The second form of overall memory training is meditation, which sometimes increases the thickness of regions that control attention and process sensory signals from the outside world. In a program that neuroscientist Amishi Jha of University of Miami calls the mindfulness-based mind-fitness training, participants build concentration by focusing on one object, such as a particular body sensation. The training, she says, has shown success in enhancing mental agility and attention "by changing brain structure and function so that brain processes are more efficient," the quality associated with intelligence.

Finally, some video games might improve general mental agility. Stan [Stan Stern of Columbia University] has trained older adults to play a complex computer-based game called Space Fortress. . . . "It requires motor control, visual search, working memory, long-term memory, and decision-making," he says. It also requires that elixir of neuroplasticity: attention. "People get better on tests of memory, motor skill, visual spatial skills, and tasks requiring cognitive flexibility," says Stern.

Meanwhile, researchers at Harvard University are embarked on a unique, long-term survey that has relevance here, concerning how we spend our time. The survey includes information on how much attention we pay to what we are doing and the impact on our happiness of what we are doing. The preliminary findings were published in the November 24, 2010, issue of the *Scientific American*, and reported in *The New York Times* on November 15, 2010 and *Psychology Today* on April 5, 2015. The article was entitled "A Wondering Mind Is An Unhappy One." The researchers, Harvard psychologists Matthew Killingsworth and Daniel Gilbert, equipped 2,200 volunteers with an applet, "Track Your Happiness," for their iPhones. They were informed that they would be contacted by text messages at random times and were requested to provide the following feedback as quickly as possible: (1) What were they doing at that moment? (2) Were they thinking about what they were doing or something else? And (3) What was their approximate happiness on a suggested scale of 1 to 10? The iPhone approach was key to retrieving the answers in real time. Recall impressions at a later time are very unreliable.

The ranking of happiness-producing levels of various activities was not especially surprising. Sex topped the list. The jaw-dropping discovery of the survey was that, excluding sex, 47 percent of the responders were thinking about something else during their activity. In other words, they were daydreaming. This means when you look at someone, you can assume that almost half the time they are thinking about something other than what they appear to be doing. The other jaw-dropper was that those paying attention were significantly happier in their activity than the daydreamers. This cut across all activities. As far as happiness was concerned, attention was more important than the activity. People assume that what they are doing or where they are, in France or outdoors, for example, determines their happiness. It does to a degree, but paying attention is more important. According to researcher Daniel Gilbert:

> Our data suggested that the location of the body is much less important than the location of the mind, and the former has surprisingly little influence on the latter. The heart goes where the mind takes it, and neither cares much about the whereabouts of the feet.

When thinking about this subject of activity, location, and happiness, I sometimes picture the cosmologist, Stephen Hawking, his twisted body in a wheelchair, introducing an episode of his television series, "Into the Universe" on the Discovery Channel: "I cannot move and must speak through a computer, [the camera zooms in on his clear blue eyes] *but in my mind I am free.*"

TRANSCENDENCE IN STUDY

This book is not a goal, but a means to a goal. That goal is a personal philosophy and, hopefully, transcendence. I believe the path to this goal, in addition to meditation, involves a type of searching, something similar to this book project that involves philosophy research and articulating my findings in writing. Often, I believed I was nearly done writing the book. But then I continued to look for new material, perhaps a different take on what I had already covered or a great new quote to add to an old section.

I don't see how you can build a personal philosophy without the discipline of documenting and re-documenting the process. Reworking parts of the book helped me remember later how I came to my current thinking, while at the same time, provided reinforcement for my beliefs.

Spinoza loved his hours of quiet study after a day of grinding lenses, and in those hours, he found his "satisfaction of mind." Colin Wilson was willing to wash dishes in the evening and sleep on the open heath so he could find the time to study in the British Museum during the day. I can't say exactly what they experienced, but in my case, there are moments so fulfilling that I feel I touch some of the transcendence of peak experiences. Karen Armstrong describes this transcendence in the study process in a recent interview[71] with Robert Wright, both of whom have published books on comparative religion. Ms. Armstrong begins by referencing her seven-year sojourn in a Catholic nunnery before leaving to become a "free-lance monotheist."

> **Armstrong**: "It was the wrong kind of prayer, the wrong kind of meditation for me." [The nunnery.]

> **Wright**: "Well, what turned out to be the right kind?"

> **Armstrong**: "For me, it's the study. When I'm reading, say the Analects [sayings of Confucius], or the Rabbis, or the Koran, or the Bible, I sometimes get touched deeply within; little miniseconds of transcendence."

> **Wright**: "So you are at least saying there is transcendence?"

---

71   http://www.onefuture.com/resources/article/robert-wright-interview-withkaren-armstrong/

Armstrong: "Transcendence has been a fact of human life. This is how we are as human beings. And we all seek to access it in one way or another."

Karen Armstrong makes two important points concerning transcendence: First, she was able to experience a form of transcendence in the process of researching spiritual writings. Second, this longing for transcendence is universal: "We all seek to access it in one way or the other." Under the mask of our popular amusements is a search for a meaning to life beyond basic survival. In Ms. Armstrong's classic, *The Great Transformation* (2006, p. xv, xvi & xxi), she discusses the modern practice of seeking transcendence outside of religion, especially in art, sporting events, and celebrity worship.

An increasing number of people find traditional religious doctrines and practices irrelevant and incredible, and turn to art, literature, dance, sport, or drugs to give them the transcendent experience that humans seem to require. We all look for moments of ecstasy and rapture, when we inhabit our humanity more fully than usual and feel deeply touched within and lifted momentarily beyond ourselves. We are meaning-seeking creatures and, unlike other animals, fall very easily into despair if we cannot find significance and value in our lives. . . . The cult of celebrity shows that we still revere models who epitomize "superhumanity." People sometimes go to great lengths to see their idols and feel an ecstatic enhancement of being in their presence. They imitate their dress and behavior.

Nigel Barber writes "The Human Beast" blog for *Psychology Today*. In a November 11, 2009, article titled, "Is Sport a Religion?" he says:

Some scholars believe that fans are highly committed to their favored stars and teams in a way that gives focus and meaning to their daily lives. In addition, sports spectatorship is a transformative experience through which fans escape their humdrum lives, just as religious experiences help the faithful to transcend their everyday existence.

The common element in the cult of celebrity is a desire for proximity to the extraordinary human, one who seems to know how to live beyond normal limitations. But my personal belief is that true transcendence does not come to you vicariously by following the experiences of celebrities.

In summary, meditation and research are both crucial parts of my journey. The former is spiritual, and the latter is analytical. The problem with getting older is that one is loaded down with tons of preconceptions. Entertaining a truly new belief becomes difficult. It's like living in a room with hundreds of old chairs that I constantly move around or re-prioritize, but nothing really changes. Yet, I sincerely believe that years of meditation and new exposure to the ideas of good philosophers have allowed me to see past some of my old preconceptions and closer to the core of the meaning. In addition, even some old ideas now shine with a new brightness, such as: all really is vanity, the past really is past, we really are more than our thoughts, and introversion is really not a sin.

So, what's left? There's more. The meditation and research described above is not enough. If we stay with just those two, we may grow in awareness and enjoy dopamine-charged moments in meditation, or great "a-ha" moments in research, but we won't have a full personal philosophy. As Thoreau put it:

> I learned this, at least, by my experiment; that if one advances confidently in the direction of his dreams, and endeavors to live the life which he has imagined, he will meet with a success unexpected in common hours. . . . In proportion as he simplifies his life, the laws of the universe will appear less complex, and solitude will not be solitude, nor poverty, poverty, nor weakness, weakness.

If you have built your castles in the air, your work need not be lost, that is where they should be. *Now put the foundations under them.* [Emphasis mine.]

—Henry David Thoreau
Walden (1854, p. 351–2)

PUTTING THE FOUNDATIONS UNDER YOUR CASTLES IN THE AIR

We are now on a path from the study of philosophical beliefs back to real life. In this we will receive no help from global-thinking philosophers like Kant and Schopenhauer. Here is where existentialism becomes helpful. It is the only major philosophy to try to relate personal beliefs to daily life in a practical manner. First, they would say, or at least Sartre would say, stop with the searching for the meaning of life from the teachings of others. You already have the power to create your own meaning. But to have real meaning, it must be authentic, that is, not some rehash of the opinions of others. I believe the two endeavors described above, meditation and liberal research, can bring you that far, in other words, to a sense of your own authenticity.

Now we must face the culmination of the process: crossing a bridge from theory back to ordinary life, but this time with a new commitment to your philosophy of life and with no excuses. This is similar to Kierkegaard's "leap of faith," except it's to a philosophy, not a religion. On the other side you no longer blame experts or other authorities and you finally accept the fact that your convictions have no ultimate proof of validity. You are just returning to where you were, but this time with an internal gyroscope of authenticity.

Nevertheless, according to Sartre, it is only through acceptance of our responsibility that we may live in authenticity. To be responsible, to live authentically, means intentionally to make choices about one's life and one's future. These choices are made most efficaciously, Sartre maintained, by becoming "engaged" in the world and by selecting a *fundamental project*,[72] a project that can mobilize and direct one's life energies and permit one to make spontaneous choices. Through the project, in short, the individual creates a world that does not yet exist and thus gives meaning to his or her life. [Italics and footnote mine.]

—Brooke Noel Moore & Kenneth Bruder
Philosophy: The Power of Ideas (2008, p. 166)

To try to illustrate a *fundamental project*, we can look to the example of Karen Armstrong, whom we quoted earlier on the subject of finding "little miniseconds of transcendence" in her research of world religions. Her research into the Axial Age convinced her that all the great religions shared one major principle. Simply put, that principle was compassion, symbolized by the Golden Rule or a variation thereof, alongside a strong commitment to self-sacrifice for the good of all. In 2008, she was awarded the $100,000 TED (Technology, Entertainment, Design Conferences) prize for her achievements and granted one wish by the organization. Her wish was help in establishing "The Charter for Compassion." She assembled a multi-faith and multinational council to write the Charter, based on the "principled determination to put ourselves in the shoes of the other . . . to build a global community where all men and women of all races, nations, and ideologies can live together in peace." A website for the organization was created so people could read the Charter and sign it. So

---

72   Sartre provides an example of a fundamental project in his novel, *La Nausée*. To recap: The central character, Roquentin, is predictably caught up in typical existential angst, which manifests itself as a persistent nausea when he reflects on his surroundings. In one shining moment, though, he is blessed with what Colin Wilson would call a peak-experience. It occurs expectantly as he overhears a recording of a blues singer performing "Some of These Days." He is infused with a burst of optimism, and later in his journal, Roquentin speculates on writing a novel that would touch the same feelings of rhythm and purpose that the music conveyed to him. Perhaps it would become his vehicle—his fundamental project for re-engaging with life.

far, more than 100,000 people have signed. The Charter for Compassion is Karen Armstrong's *fundamental project.* "Through this project, in short, the individual creates a world that does not yet exist and thus gives meaning to his or her life."

In other words, a philosophy of life needs to incorporate purposeful action in addition to contemplation. Sartre believed that your choices and actions, if they were based on authentic beliefs would, by definition, be sincere and bring about positive Meaning, not only to your own life but to all mankind in an otherwise meaningless world. Or, as Emerson put it in *Self Reliance*: "To believe that what is true for you in your private heart is true for all men—that is genius." Focusing in on a fundamental project could provide structure to this quest for meaning and put "the foundation under . . . your castles in the sky."

※

Note From the Author: Reviews are gold to authors! If you've enjoyed this book, would you please consider rating it and reviewing it on www. amazon.com?

APPENDIX

EXISTENTIALISM

No summary of non-analytic philosophy, even one as short as this book's, should be complete without examining the best-known modern philosophical movement: existentialism. It is being treated here, though, as an addendum to the central idealistic philosophies of Plato, Spinoza, Schopenhauer, and others. Existentialists have very little use for idealism or for metaphysics in general. If you are going to have a working personal philosophy, I do not see how it could include both traditional idealistic philosophies and the central core of existentialism, which rejects these traditional philosophies. Holding both views would be, in my opinion, contradictory. Also, I believe peak experiences resonate better with an idealistic philosophy.

Not only does existentialism reject the metaphysics of earlier philosophies and the Axial Age, but also its base beliefs, at least as described by Jean-Paul Sartre, strike me as bizarre as Nietzsche's "Superman." Of course, it's possible that Sartre's philosophy is just beyond my cognitive abilities.[73] Sartre in his most significant non-fiction book, *Being and Nothingness* (1943), begins

---

73   When I have really tried to understand something but couldn't, most of the time it turned out later that it wasn't true to begin with.

with his base belief that humans, alone among all species, have the power to "nihilate" anything and everything. For example, one could decide categorically that there was no moon and act accordingly. People could try to point it out in the sky, and you would see nothing. Then for you, holding Sartre's conviction, there really would be no moon. Going further, Sartre argued that this power to nihilate and create a nothingness could belong only to an entity that was itself a nothingness.[74]

> The being [you and me] by which nothingness arrives in the world must nihilate nothingness [deny the existence of our species's unique ability] in our being, and even so it runs the risk of establishing nothingness as a transcendent in the very heart of immanence [the inauthentic, bourgeois lives of common man].
>
> —Jean-Paul Sartre
> *Being and Nothingness* (1943)

Sartre seems to be saying that while having the power to create nothingness can be useful, we must deny the existence of this power, or our lives would be forever changed. We might realize that we, too, at our core are a nothingness. This is the part I find bizarre. But a few brave souls are willing to transcend this denial by embracing the terrifying power of choice, uncertainty, and self-responsibility of being, at our core, a "bubble of nothingness."

Whatever the truth of Sartre's belief about our being bubbles of nothingness, we should move on to examine this fascinating philosophy in more detail. Existentialists have a strong conviction that much of the information fed to

---

74   I can stay with Sartre up to a point. Sartre provides us with an example in *Being and Nothingness*. He is waiting for his friend, Pierre, in a Parisian cafe. He is able to determine that Pierre has not yet arrived by scanning the cafe and then deciding to create a "non-Pierre," thereby nihilating him. I can entertain the proposition that we have this power and are the only species with this power. I am left behind, though, by the jump of logic that this power could be possessed only by a being that is itself a nothingness.

us by others is for their self-aggrandizing purposes, like the projectionists in Plato's Cave. Everyone is included in this self-aggrandizing lot, including philosophers, and even existentialists. An example would be a philosopher who was more concerned about his reputation than the unvarnished truth and would disseminate a message to the public with an eye to which spin would most enhance his or her reputation. Instead of depending on others, existentialists believe you must create your own philosophy out of whole cloth. For these purposes, the opinions of philosophers and others are worthless. The only real meaning you will ever find must come from within.

People who become existentialists usually begin with a perplexing feeling of angst. The best-known character in literature to experience existential angst is Hamlet, the central character in Shakespeare's play. Hamlet faces a major dilemma. He has evidence that his uncle, Claudius, has murdered his father, the King of Denmark. With the old king out of the way, Claudius now claims the throne and marries the Queen, Hamlet's mother. Someone other than Hamlet might have followed the path of immanence or "bad faith"[75] by quickly dispatching Claudius—because that fit society's code of honor of avenging one's father or perhaps because trusted aides in the court recommended it. But then the play would have had a very short run.[76]

---

75 "Bad faith" is Sartre's term for not acting according to your personal consciousness and avoiding responsibility by following instead the dictates and opinions of others. It is not that people of bad faith don't face conflicting choices. For example, a teenage boy might crave trendy clothes to impress his peers. He comes across just the right items in a store, but they are more than he can afford. The choice is to leave the store or to shoplift. The conflict is between the improved status the clothes might bring with his friends against the disapproval shoplifting will bring (if caught) in his adult community. Either choice is "bad faith" because it is motivated by the opinions of others.

76 *Hamlet* had already been performed on stage by a different playwright as recently as ten years earlier. It was based on a popular legend about a twelfth-century Danish prince. In that legend the prince is set on a path of righteous vengeance from the very beginning. Shakespeare's *Hamlet* confounded his audiences—who knew what he was supposed to do—yet he vacillated and engaged in introspective soliloquies. "With *Hamlet*, a play poised midway between a religious [and honor-bound] past and a secular future, Shakespeare finally found a dramatically compelling way to internalize contesting forces; the essay-like soliloquy proved to be the perfect vehicle . . . to confront issues . . . that defied easy solution." James Shapiro, *A Year in the Life of William Shakespeare 1599*, (2005) p.301.

Shakespeare is on to something much more interesting—his Hamlet would embody the conflicting worldviews about religion and honor in 1599 that the audience was experiencing firsthand. His indecision is excruciatingly painful to the point of considering suicide. The passages below are from Shakespeare's *Hamlet*.

> To be or not to be—that is the question.

Hamlet wonders if he even has the right as an individual to choose "not to be." The Church clearly believes he does not have that right.

> O, that this too solid flesh would melt
>   Thaw and resolve itself into a dew!
> Or that the Everlasting [God] had not fix'd
>   His cannon 'gainst self-slaughter! O God! O God!

Perhaps there was another authority he could look to help him decide whether to choose suicide and/or to kill Claudius. What would society consider appropriate to demonstrate a noble sense of honor or of ethical behavior?

> Whether 'tis nobler in the mind to suffer
>   The slings and arrows of outrageous fortune
> Or to take arms against a sea of troubles
>   And by opposing end them? To die: to sleep;

> To sleep: perchance to dream: ay there's the rub.

The Church says no to suicide. Hamlet then briefly considers what could be considered noble action, but suicide still seems appealing. What about reasoning out an answer? Unfortunately, his reasoning reminds him that while suicide might allow him to escape, he might also wake up in some "undiscovered country from whose bourn no traveller returns." He is now more uncertain than ever.

> Thus conscience does make cowards of us all;
> And thus the native hue of resolution
> Is sicklied over with the pale cast of thought,

Hamlet finally does kill Claudius, but it happens haphazardly in a fencing match with Laertes in which the King, the Queen, Laertes, and Hamlet all die. This occurs before Hamlet has come to any conscious decision about what he should do. The moral for the existentialist is that Hamlet had the authentic power individually to kill Claudius and/or himself all along, but that was something he could not accept. The authentic power to choose for oneself transcends the dictates of religion, social morality, or rationality. At least, though, Hamlet would not allow himself the easy way out, or follow the path of immanence, by acting according to what he thought society believed in order to lessen his responsibility.

Like Hamlet, our acceptance of the full implication of our power of choice is so difficult that it often has to be a two-step process. First is that famous feeling of existential angst. We know something is wrong; we just don't know what. Accompanying this angst is the feeling that much of what we have been told or taught by others is meaningless. Many of the characters in the novels and plays by existentialists experience this angst and meaninglessness. Some describe it as something physically present, like an odor that can bring on nausea in one's body. This makes the uncertainty more menacing: an unknown evil that can manifest itself in the real world.

Often in these novels and plays, the growing unease is punctuated by brief episodes of breathtaking beauty or sudden clarity and meaning. Unfortunately, these episodes only accentuate the contrast between what could be and the hollowness of the other 99 percent of life.

Eventually some people will find a way to transcend the meaninglessness of life and create their own meaning out of nothing. This is by no means automatic. The second step in the process is coming to grips with one's mortality. We all unapologetically live in a state of denial. Talk about procrastination! We would do anything to avoid thinking about our inevitable death. Oh, we know about it on one level; otherwise, we wouldn't write wills. But, if we really accepted it on a core level, we would act differently by not pretending to be immortal. Martin Heidegger (1889–1976) deals with this issue in his masterpiece, *Sein und Zeit* (*Being and Time*) (1927). In the following passage from *Irrational Man* (1958, p. 225), William Barrett summarizes Heidegger's view of our belief about death.

> Men die. This happens every day in the world. Death is a public event in the world, of which we take notice in obituaries; we pay the necessary social obsequies and are sometimes deeply touched emotionally. But, so long as death remains a fact outside ourselves, we have not yet passed from the proposition "Men die" to the proposition "I am to die."
>
> Only by taking my death into myself, according to Heidegger, does an authentic existence become possible for me. . . . Though terrifying, the taking of death into ourselves is also liberating: It frees us from servitude to the petty cares that threaten to engulf our daily lives and thereby opens us to the essential projects by which we can make our lives personally and significantly our own.

The coming to terms with death is sometimes suddenly forced on people. Fyodor Dostoyevsky (1821–1881), author and existentialist, had such a coming to terms. He found himself one day standing before a firing squad, facing certain and imminent death. Then he was inexplicably given a reprieve at the last possible moment. It was the seminal moment of his life and drove him, Kierkegaard-like, into the arms of the Russian Orthodox Church. As the time from this very moment to certain death grows short, the value of life grows exponentially.[77] Or, as Private Joker puts it in Stanley Kubrick's *Full Metal Jacket* (1987): "The dead know only one thing: it is better to be alive."

JEAN-PAUL SARTRE (1905–1980)

Jean-Paul Sartre faced imminent death while also experiencing the ultimate power of the state to prescribe precisely how its citizens should live. This occurred during the German occupation of France in the early 1940s and his time with the French underground. This is how he described the experience:

> We had lost all our rights, beginning with the right to speak. Every day we were insulted to our faces and had to take it in silence. Under one pretext or another, as workers, as Jews, or political prisoners, we were exported en masse. Everywhere, on billboards, in the newspapers, on the [movie] screen, we encountered the revolting and insipid pictures of ourselves that our oppressors wanted us to accept. . . . Exile, captivity, and especially death (which we usually shrink from facing at all in happier times) became for us the habitual objects of our concern. . . . And the choice that each

---

77 Dostoyevsky retells his own story in *The Idiot* (1868–9) through a fictional character who also faced a firing squad, recalling his thoughts during what he thought were his last five minutes on earth. "He recounted that those five minutes were like an eternity to him, a priceless treasure. . . . 'What if I were not to die! What if I were to have my life back again—a whole infinity! And all would be mine! I would make every moment last for ages, nothing would be wasted, every moment would be accounted for, everything would be taken care of!' He confessed that eventually this thought incensed him so much that he wished they would hurry up and shoot him." (p. 63)

of us made of his life was an authentic choice because it was made face to face with death, because it could always be expressed in these terms:

'Rather death than. . . .'

—Jean-Paul Sartre

The Republic of Silence essay (1944)

What Sartre found in his life with an underground literary group during the occupation[78]—when he felt his life was at risk every moment—was that his authentic choices became clear. For us, though, living in "happier times," our authentic choices are not only not clear, but we will "nihilate" even consideration of what those choices may mean.

For example, a high school student is a witness to unjust bullying. There are all sorts of first-line defenses to protect the student from risking involvement: leaving the scene, or rationalizing others will stop it or that the victim is partially to blame. But the best defense, which can reliably protect the student from all ambiguous situations, is to have no internal and authentic opinion about what "unjust" means. Having an opinion may involve the student in some hairy situations that could put his security and popularity at risk and could result in unpredictable outcomes. For instance, assume in this example the student is the exception and does hold an authentic view on the meaning of injustice and confronts the bullies. The student successfully stops the bullying, but the school administration hears of the instance and suspends the bullies. Most, including the student, believe the suspensions are a severe overreaction. Nevertheless, the brave student would have to accept part of the blame. It's easier *not* to be an existentialist.

---

78   My image of Sartre in the French Resistance blowing up German installations is a bit misguided. He did contribute to a clandestine newspaper called *Combat* edited by Albert Camus. "According to Camus, Sartre was a writer who resisted, not a resistor who wrote." (Wikipedia)

A few people, like Sartre and Dostoyevsky, discovered their authentic beliefs or their internal gyroscope in response to very trying circumstances that bordered on death. We might envy the conviction of their philosophy, but have not ourselves faced similar near-death conditions that might engender such conviction.

Or perhaps we are just too weak on our own to embrace existentialism. Some existentialists believe that at one time we found the conviction we needed in Christianity, but that science and the growth of materialism robbed us of our faith.

> Religion to medieval man was not so much a theological system as a solid psychological matrix surrounding the individual's life from birth to death, sanctifying and enclosing all its ordinary and extraordinary occasions [baptism, marriage ceremony, funeral, etc.] in sacrament and ritual. . . . In losing religion, man lost the concrete connection with a transcendent realm of being; he was set free to deal with this world in all its brute objectivity. . . . Henceforth, in seeking his own completeness man would have to do for himself what he once had done for him, unconsciously, by the Church through its sacramental life.
>
> —William Barrett
> *Irrational Man* (1962, pp. 24–25)

The erosion of Christianity and the rise of secularism took place over centuries, so slowly that Europe was unaware of anything being lost. Finally, the alarm was sounded by Nietzsche when he declared "God is dead" (*The Gay Science*, 1888). Although he was overly dramatic, he did think it was imperative that people take notice. He hoped his fellow man would wake up and realize the fact that in their day men could call themselves Christians and still be spiritually bankrupt. A man's outward lip service and regular church attendance would be meaningless if God had been cut out of his heart by a greater faith in science and materiality. One cannot truly serve two gods.

By his very public pronouncements, Nietzsche set himself adrift from a society more interested in preserving the status quo than engaging in soul-searching. This isolation may have helped to unhinge him later in life. Kierkegaard shared Nietzsche's belief in society's spiritual bankruptcy but called on his generation to wake up to their lost spirituality and make a "leap of faith" back to the life of the true Christian believer.

The philosophy of Plato, Spinoza, and others was concerned with essence: the true nature of things and of us. Existentialists believe that philosophy, essence, and ideology don't mean anything when one's existence is at stake; hence existence comes before essence. An episode near the end of Ernest Hemingway's *For Whom the Bell Tolls* (1940, p. 321) illustrates this. The scene takes place near Madrid close to the end of the Spanish Civil War. A group of leftist Republicans are making a last stand on a hillside during the siege of Madrid. Franco's warplanes have spotted their position and are approaching for a bombing run. Joaquín, to calm his nerves, begins to chant out loud some of the inspirational sayings of his Communist heroine and philosopher, Pasionaria. But, as the roar of the warplanes grows louder, he abruptly reverts to his childhood religion.

> "Pasionaria says 'Better to die on thy——' " Joaquín was saying to himself as the drone came nearer. Then he shifted suddenly into "Hail Mary, full of grace, the Lord is with thee; Blessed art thou among women and Blessed is the fruit of thy womb, Jesus. Holy Mary, Mother of God, pray for us sinners now and at the hour of our death. . . . [Then] he remembered quickly as the roar came now unbearably and started an act of contrition racing in it, "Oh my God, I am heartily sorry for having offended thee who art worthy of all my love——"

When in the course of our lives we turn for help in understanding our condition, we are much more likely to turn to religion than to philosophy. Why? Because religion offers answers with conviction, while philosophy offers general theories. But if we don't like the religion's answers, we are set adrift. Existentialism, more than any other philosophy, deals with issues we really face in life and deals with them in a personal way. It also gives us the opportunity to see how the decisions we make as individuals can make an important difference to the world, at least symbolically. We come to realize that our decisions are not as mundane as we thought. We are in an existential struggle to bring meaning to our lives and, by extension, to all of humankind. Our struggle is no greater, or lesser, than anyone else's. This is no trifling matter. Finally, existentialism teaches us that we are not as hemmed in by convention and society as we might like to believe. Out of that bubble of nothing in our core, we retain the power, even now, to make amazing changes in our lives. But we must act now because our opportunity could end by accident, tomorrow, underneath a bus. As Thomas Wartenberg in *Existentialism* (2008, p. 171) puts it:

"After all, this is the one shot you have at life. . . . Why not live it as an Existentialist?"

REFERENCES

Armstrong, Karen and Robert Wright. 2010. Robert Wright interview with Karen Armstrong. http://www.onefuture.com/resources/article/robert-wright-interview-with-karenarmstrong/. October 17, 2010.

Armstrong, Karen. 2006. *The Great Transformation*. New York: Anchor Books.

Barber, Nigel. 2009. "Is Sport a Religion?" The Human Beast blog for *Psychology Today,* November 11, 2009.

Barrett, William. 1962. *Irrational Man*. New York: Anchor Books.

Begley, Sharon. 2011. "Can You Build a Better Brain?" *Newsweek* (January 10 & 17, 2011).

Bogle, John. 2013. *Frontline* interview hosted by Martin Smith on PBS April 13, 2013, for "The Retirement Gamble," episode.

Bourdieu, Pierre. 1987. *Distinction: A Social Critique of the Judgment of Taste*. Translated by Richard Nice. Cambridge, MA: Harvard University Press.

Bourget, David and David Chalmers. 2009. The PhilPaper Survey. November 2009. http://philpapers.org/surveys/.

Brynjolfsson, Erik and Andrew McAfee. 2011. *Race Against The Machine.* Lexington, MA: Digital Frontier Press.

Cain, Susan. 2012. *Quiet, The Power of Introversion in a World That Can't Stop Talking.* New York: Random House.

Campbell, Joseph. 1962. *The Masks of God: Oriental Mythology,* New York: Penguin Books.

Camus, Albert. 1942. *The Stranger.* New York: Vantage Press.

Carnegie, Dale. 1936. *How to Win Friends and Influence People.* New York: Pocket Books.

Cooper, James Fenimore. 1840. *The Pathfinder.* New York: Dodd, Mead & Company.

Dostoyevsky, Fyodor, 1869. *The Idiot.* Translated by Ignat Avsey. 2010. Surrey, UK. Oneworld Classics.

Durant, Will. 1926. *The Story of Philosophy,* New York: Simon & Schuster.

Emerson, Ralph Waldo. 1841. "Self-Reliance." *Essays: First Series.*

———. 1860–66. *Journals and Miscellaneous Notebook, vol. 15.*

Erikson, Stephen. 2006. *Philosophy as a Guide to Living.* Chantilly, VA: The Teaching Company.

Freud, Sigmund. 1933. *New Introductory Lectures on Psycho-Analysis.* New York: W. W. Norton & Co.

Galbraith, John Kenneth. 1958. *The Affluent Society.* Boston: Houghton Mifflin.us

Goethe. 1970. *Faust.* Translated by Barker Farley. Toronto: University of Toronto Press.

Ghilarducci, Teresa. 2008. *When I'm Sixty-Four*. Princeton, NJ: Princeton University Press.

Gottlieb, Anthony. 2010. *Intelligent Life* magazine, Spring 2010.

Grazia, Sebastian de. 1962. *Of Time, Work and Leisure*. New York: Vintage Books.

Hall, Edward T. 1959. *The Silent Language*. New York: Doubleday.

Hanh, Thich Nhat. 1975. *Mindfulness, An Introduction to the Practice of Meditation*. Boston: Beacon Press

Heidegger, Martin. 1946. *Poetry, Language, Thought*. 1971. Translated by Albert Hofsdadter. New York: HarperCollins.

———. 1927. *Sein und Zeit (Being and Time)*.

Hemingway, Ernest. 1940. *For Whom the Bell Tolls*. New York: Charles Scribner's Sons.

Hoffer, Eric. 1951. *True Believer: Thoughts on the Nature of Mass Movements*. New York: Harper.

Jaspers, Karl. 1953. *The Origin and Goal of History*. New Haven, CT: Yale University Press.

Jung, Carl G. 1938. *Psychology and Religion*. New Haven, CT: Yale University Press.

Keynes, John Maynard. 1930. "Economic Possibilities for our Grandchildren." In J.M. Keynes, *Essays in Persuasion*. London: Macmillan.

Killingsworth, Matthew A. and Daniel T. Gilbert. 2001. "A Wondering Mind Is An Unhappy One." November 24, 2010, *Scientific American*.

Kubrick, Stanley. 1987. Movie: *Full Metal Jacket*. Based on Gustav Hasford's *The Short-Timers* (1979).

Lazar, Sara. 2006. "Meditation Found to Increase Brain Size." *Harvard Gazette*, February 2006.

Levine, Jeff and Lea Steele. 2005. "The Transcendent Experience," *Explore.*

Linder, Staffan B. 1970. *The Harried Leisure Class.* New York: Columbia University Press.

Mann, Thomas. 1938. *Schopenhauer.* Stockholm: BermannFisher.

Marx, Karl. 1875. "In Critique of the Gatha Programme." *Die Neue Zeit.*

Maslow, Abraham H. 1970. *Religion, Values and Peak-Experiences.* New York: Penguin.

Mead, Margaret (ed.). 1953. *Cultural Patterns and Technical Change.* Paris: UNESCO.

Mill, John Stuart. 1863. *Utilitarianism.*

Moore, Brooke Noel and Kenneth Bruder. 2011. *Philosophy: The Power of Ideas.* New York: McGraw-Hill.

Nichols, Ashton. 2006. *Emerson, Thoreau, and the Transcendentalist Movement.* Chantilly, VA: The Teaching Company.

Nin, Anaïs. 1961. *Seduction of the Minotaur,* Chicago.

Packard, Vance. 1959. *The Status Seekers.* New York: Pocket Books.

Phelps, Edmund S. 2010. "Corporations and Keynes: His Philosophy of Growth." *Revisiting Keynes* (2010, p. 101) ed. by Lorenzo Pecchi and Gustavo Piga. London: The MIT Press.

Pieper, Joseph. 1948. *Leisure, The Basis of Culture.* Translated by Roger Scruton. 1998. South Bend: St. Augustine's Press.

Retry, Robert. 1998. "Schopenhauer." *A Companion to Continental Philosophy,* edited by Simon Critchley and William R. Schroeder. Oxford, UK: Blackwell Publishers.

Robertson, Daniel N. 2004. *Great Ideas of Philosophy, 2nd Edition*. Chantilly, VA: The Teaching Company.

Rosenbaum, Eric. 2012. *The Street*, March 15, 2012. www. thestreet.com

Rowe, Jonathan. 2003. "Wasted Time, Wasted Work," *Take Back Your Time* (pp. 58–65), ed. by John de Graaf. San Francisco: Berrett-Koehler Publishers.

Safranski, Rüdiger. 1991. *Schopenhauer and the Wild Years of Philosophy*. Cambridge, MA: Harvard University Press.

Sartre, Jean-Paul. 1943. "Being and Nothingness" essay.

———. 1947. "The Republic of Silence" essay.

———. 1949. "*La Nausée*." essay.

Schor, Juliet 2003. "The (Even More) Overworked American." *Take Back Your Time*, John de Graaf, Editor. San Francisco: Berrett-Koehler Publishers.

———. 1992. *The Overworked American*. New York: Basic Books.

———. 1998. *The Overspent American*. New York: HarperCollinsPublishers.

———. 2004. *Born to Buy*. New York: Scribner.

Shapiro, James. 2005. *A Year in the Life of William Shakespeare 1559*. New York: Harper Perennial.

Shirer, William L. 1960. *The Rise and Fall of the Third Reich*. New York: Simon & Schuster.

Skidelsky, Robert & Edward. 2012. *How Much Is Enough?* New York: Other Press.

Stiglitz, Joseph E. 2010. "Toward a General Theory of Consumerism: Reflections on Keynes's "Economic Possibilities for our Grandchildren." *Revisiting Keynes*. 2010. ed. by Lorenzo Pecchi and Gustavo Piga. London: The MIT Press.

Strathern, Paul. 2001. *Wittgenstein*. London: Harper Press. Thomas, Henry. 1962. *Understanding the Great Philosophers*. Garden City, NY: Doubleday.

Thoreau, Henry David. 1854. *Walden*, New Haven, CT: Yale University Press.

Tietjens, Eunice. 1922. "The Most-Sacred Mountain." *The Second Book of Modern Verse*, ed. by Jessie B. Rittenhouse.

Tillich, Paul. 1959. *Theology of Culture*, New York: Oxford University Press.

Twain, Mark. 1967. Portrayed by Hal Holbrook, "Mark Twain Tonight." CBS.

Unknown. 2013. "Stop 401(k) Fees From Cheating You Out of Retirement Money." *Consumer Reports*, August, 2013.

Veblen, Thorstein. 1899. *Theory of the Leisure Class*. New York: B.W. Huebsch.

Wartenberg, Thomas. 2008. *Existentialism*. Oxford, UK: Oneworld Publications.

Waxman, Barbara and Robert A. Mendelson. 2006. *How to Love Your Retirement*. Atlanta: Hundreds of Heads Books.

Wikipedia. 2013. "Research on Meditation." Last modified 26 August 2013. http://en.wikipedia.org/wiki/Research_on_meditation

Williams, Terry Tempest. 1991. *Refuge*, New York: Pantheon Books.

Wilson, Colin. 1956. *The Outsider*. Los Angeles: Jeremy P. Tarcher, Inc.

————. 1994. "Colin Wilson on Peak Experiences." *You Tube*. www.youtube.com/watch?v=bNpJo:UaRK.

————. 2009. *Super Consciousness.*. London: Watkins Publishing.

Wittgenstein, Ludwig. 1922. *Tractatus Logico-Philosophicus*.

Yeats, W. B. 1950. "Vacillation." *Poems of the Underground*. London: London Underground.

ACKNOWLEDGEMENT

The historical description of the great philosophers—starting with Bacon and ending with Kant—was based on the chronological framework provided by Will Durant in *The Story of Philosophy* (1926). For his nonpareil contribution to general public understanding of the great philosophers, we all owe him a debt of gratitude. Readers interested in the pursuit of amateur philosophy would do well to begin with his classic.

I'm very grateful to book shepherd Shel Horowitz of frugalmarketing .com, who had the vision to see the much more powerful book than the one I thought I was writing, and to walk me through the complex path of creating a well-edited, well-designed, well-titled, and impactful book. Our allies in the designing and editing phases were Michele DeFilippo and Ronda Rawlins of 1106 Design. They do great work!

INDEX

ABOUT THE AUTHOR

Forrest Wright is a retired certified financial planner (CFP) and holds an MBA degree from The Wharton School, University of Pennsylvania. Articles about his prior work as a money manager have appeared in *The New York Times, The Financial Anaylsts Journal, Newsday,* and other national publications.

Forrest has extensive experience in retirement planning. In fact, at age eight he asked his father, in 1946, how much money he would need not to have to work. His father answered, "Two million," and Forrest's quest began. However, his real interest was not in the $2,000,000, or not working, but in something he discovered outside of work.